W9-ASR-714

Praise for *Culture Rules*

"Mark Miller has put together a comprehensive collection of advice around the most elusive aspect of business success. Every leader will no doubt find something valuable in *Culture Rules* to apply to their organization."

—Patrick Lencioni, *New York Times* Bestselling Author,
The Five Dysfunctions of a Team

"When I speak to companies about what it takes to build a strong, winning culture, the expert I point to the most as an example is . . . Mark Miller. For decades, he's been leading the charge on building cultures that scale, cultures that serve, and cultures that succeed. This book takes what can often be a fuzzy topic, culture, and clarifies it with tactical practical advice that will improve your organization today. Culture is the hardest thing to build and the easiest thing to lose. Give you and your team a secret weapon. Read this book!"

—Jon Acuff, *New York Times* Bestselling Author,
Soundtracks: The Surprising Solution to Overthinking

"Today's top talent are selecting organizations based on culture and the potential to grow and develop, both professionally and personally. In *Culture Rules*, Mark Miller provides the framework to create and sustain a world-class culture for any organization, regardless of size. Leaders who desire to create and implement an authentic culture that has the ability to adapt and thrive must read and apply the lessons Mark provides in *Culture Rules*."

—Andrew Cox, Chief of Staff and Vice President
of Leadership Development, Wellstar Health System

"The right culture is foundational to the success of any business. Mark skillfully guides leaders to the achievement of a differentiated and impactful institutional culture."

—Julie Charlestein, CEO Premier Dental Products and
Author of *How to Lead Your Family Business*

"For leaders looking to create a winning culture within your organization, *Culture Rules* is your answer. Mark Miller touches on every aspect in this book for leaders to have a thriving culture. I've seen it firsthand when I put some of these concepts into action within my organization. This book is the real deal, and I recommend it to all leaders!"

—Tyrone Oliver, Commissioner, Georgia Department of Juvenile Justice

"I've been a fan of Mark Miller for years and have loved all his books. *Culture Rules* combines Mark's decades of leadership experience; a multiyear, multimillion-dollar study on organizational culture; and listening to thousands of global leaders to unearth the universal truths about building High Performance Cultures. This book is a game changer!"

—Tommy Spaulding, *New York Times* Bestselling Author of *The Heart-Led Leader* and *The Gift of Influence*

"Far too many leaders assume that organizations with great cultures are soft on performance. Mark Miller makes the case in *Culture Rules* that nothing could be further from the truth. High Performance Cultures enable people and their organization to win. Read this book and change your world!"

—Ryan Leak, Executive Coach, Communicator, and Author of *Chasing Failure*

"It's been said that culture eats strategy for lunch. How's yours? Any gaps? Can it be better? After leading for more than forty years in one of the world's great organizations, Mark Miller has written the definitive work on how to create a High Performance Culture—one where the people and the organization both win! *Culture Rules* will unlock yours and your team's greatness."

—Todd Duncan, *New York Times* Bestselling Author, *High Trust Selling: Make More Money in Less Time with Less Stress*

"*Culture Rules* provides a practical road map for human-centered leaders to build stronger cultures. Whether you're an executive working to influence large-scale change or a team leader working to build a great culture on your team, this book will inspire your thinking and give you easy-to-implement approaches to build the culture you need."

—Karin Hurt, CEO of Let's Grow Leaders and Author of *Courageous Cultures*

Culture Rules

CULTURE
RULES

The Leader's Guide to Creating
the Ultimate Competitive Advantage

MARK MILLER

Matt Holt Books
An Imprint of BenBella Books, Inc.
Dallas, TX

Matt Holt is an imprint of BenBella Books, Inc.
10440 N. Central Expressway
Suite 800
Dallas, TX 75231
benbellabooks.com
Send feedback to feedback@benbellabooks.com

BenBella and *Matt Holt* are federally registered trademarks.

Printed in the United States of America
10 9 8 7 6 5 4 3 2

Library of Congress Control Number: 2022035849
ISBN 9781637742877 (hardcover)
ISBN 9781637742884 (electronic)

Editing by Katie Dickman
Copyediting by Lydia Choi
Proofreading by Lisa Story and Marissa Wold Uhrina
Indexing by WordCo Indexing Services, Inc.
Author photo by Mary Caroline Russell
Text design and composition by Jordan Koluch
Cover design by Brigid Pearson
Cover image © Shutterstock / BLAGORODEZ
Printed by Lake Book Manufacturing

Special discounts for bulk sales are available.
Please contact bulkorders@benbellabooks.com.

To Beau, Jim, Alan, Lance, David, Matt, Mike, Randy, and Frank: thanks for your endless encouragement and ongoing prayers. I'm not yet the leader I want to be, but thanks to you, I am better than I used to be.

Contents

Rule #3: Adapt

Game On!

LEADERS ANIMATE CULTURE

*I came to see, in my time at IBM, that culture isn't just
an aspect of the game—it is the game.*
—**Lou Gerstner, Former CEO of IBM**

Welcome to the game!

Have you ever considered why some games are compelling, even captivating, while others are quickly abandoned due to boredom or fatigue? The answer is found in the concept of the magic circle.

The magic circle dates back to 1938, when Dutch historian Johan Huizinga wrote about the impact of play on culture. Here's the basic idea: if you can create a space, a "magic circle," in which people can enter and immerse themselves fully in a game, the activities within that game will become approachable, engaging, and even fun.[1]

To do this well requires a very intentional effort on the part of the game designer to establish the rules, boundaries, and other parameters of this new world—the magic circle. To begin the game, the participants are often asked to suspend judgment and set aside their preconceived notions as they enter the circle.

An example of this I believe many of you have experienced firsthand is the board game Monopoly.

When you agree to play a game like Monopoly, you accept the rules, conditions, and boundaries established by the creators of the game. I'm guessing the first time you played, someone explained the basics before you began. You didn't know everything in the beginning, but you learned enough to get started.

You were clear on the objective, the role of the players, and the game pieces you would use. You also were willing to suspend judgment to some extent: you knew the money changing hands was not real and the real estate deeds you coveted, like Park Place and Boardwalk, were not actual assets. If you received notification that you must Go to Jail, you would, but you didn't expect to languish there long, and you didn't need a lawyer to argue your case to be released. The person playing the role of the banker was almost assuredly not qualified to be a banker, yet you decided to play nevertheless.

As you played, your confidence and competence improved. As a result, your engagement level likely increased as well. And, if your experience was typical, you probably invested several hours of your time. Depending on those you played with, chances are high you even had fun. This is the power of the game, the magic circle in action.

For our purposes, building a thriving High Performance Culture is the game, and leaders are the designers. I want this book to serve as your guide to building your own magic circle. In essence, that is what your culture is. A place, physical or virtual, where you set the parameters in which people work. A place where the organization establishes the rules of conduct and its values, how the game will be played, the options and variables in play, the desired activities and boundaries that govern the game, and more.

YOUR CHALLENGE

In 2005, American professor, philosopher, and novelist David Foster Wallace gave the commencement address for Kenyon College. He began his remarks with this story.

"There are these two young fish swimming along, and they happen to meet an older fish swimming the other way who nods at them and says, 'Morning, boys. How's the water?' And the two young fish swim on for a bit, and then eventually one of them looks over at the other and goes, 'What the hell is water?'"[2]

In this brief anecdote, Wallace captured one of the primary challenges with culture: because leaders are immersed in it, they often have trouble seeing it. As a consequence of this blindness, many cannot even begin to fathom the impact their culture is having on their organizations.

Yet, whether a leader is keenly aware of or oblivious to the impact of culture in and of itself does nothing to mitigate its effect. When culture is seen, understood, and intentionally crafted by leaders, it is the ultimate force for good in an organization—"good" as defined by energy, engagement, retention, performance, and competitive advantage.

There is nothing in an organization that has the reach, scope, and impact of culture other than the leaders who create it.

Culture is a beast—the question is, Has the beast been tamed, its immense power harnessed for good, or does it terrorize the inhabitants of the realm?

OUR TEAM'S CHALLENGE

To explore the topic of culture, I had the opportunity to build an amazing team—a diverse group of wicked-smart people from both the marketplace and academia. The challenge our team embraced was audacious:

> To help leaders around the world create
> their own High Performance Cultures.

To realize this goal, we talked to or surveyed more than six thousand men and women. They came from ten countries around the world and represented senior leaders, mid-level leaders, and frontline workers. These leaders and their organizations are the heroes of this book. We will tell their stories and learn from both their successes and shortcomings.

As we began to dive in, we realized the watery nature of this thing we call culture was only one of many challenges leaders face.

- The "water" that is culture contains a lot more than hydrogen and oxygen—there are literally scores of drivers and interdependencies.
- It's difficult to work on something you cannot see.
- Every culture is unique and therefore needs different types of support.

- Culture is a never-ending responsibility requiring continual attention.
- For most leaders, culture is a stated priority but not an operational one; its ownership is often delegated to others.

Honestly, we documented many other challenges, too. I dare not mention them all here or you would probably stop reading and throw up your hands in frustration, overwhelmed by the apparent futility of it all. You might assume, given the enormity and complexity of the task, the topic of culture is unassailable. You would be wrong.

During our exploration, we discovered a few simple rules—three, to be exact—that any leader who wants to master the game of culture craft must abide by to be successful.

When these culture rules are followed consistently, you can create a fully engaged workforce; when ignored or poorly followed, boredom, mediocrity, and disengagement become the norm. When these latter conditions persist, people will quit your game and look for another to join.

THE PROMISE OF THIS BOOK

You can create your own magic circle! You can create a compelling and fulfilling place for people to work. However, I want to set the proper expectations for you. This book does not contain a one-size-fits-all approach to building culture. As I said earlier, every culture is unique.

Before we explore the path ahead, I want to provide a little more context. These are some of the things I wish I had known as a young leader about to enter the game for the first time.

- Culture influences everything that happens in your organization. That's why culture rules!
- The stakes of this game are extremely high. They include the health and vitality of the organization you serve, the performance of the enterprise, the stewardship of the people, your competitive place in your market, and your legacy as a leader.
- This game is governed by your free will. You can play, pretend, or squander your opportunity—it's totally your call.
- Every leader in the world is capable of playing well . . . if they want to.

In our first section, we'll begin as many game instructions do: with an overview of the Game Basics, including a more detailed description of the game, the components, what you can do, the consequences if you don't, and the endgame.

After the Game Basics, we'll devote a section to each of the three culture rules that govern play in any organization. Those who don't know the rules, ignore the rules, or violate them, intentionally or unintentionally, will never play the game well; some will even be disqualified. We will look at several real-world examples so you can see the rules in action and begin to think about how you might apply them in your organization.

Following the introduction of each rule, we'll devote several chapters to the moves you can make to build and enhance the culture of your organization.

The final section is titled "Game On!" In it, I'll introduce you to one of history's most courageous leaders and share final thoughts to help you apply what you have learned on our journey together.

ARE YOU READY TO PLAY?

In every organization, people either love their work or loathe it; they contribute or coast. Your culture can be soul enriching or soul crushing. Your culture gives life or takes it. Your employees care deeply or could not care less. Your organization's culture can become the most valuable non-tangible asset you steward. You can build a High Performance Culture—a place where people and the organization win.

Sound too good to be true? Well, there is a catch: cultures like the ones I'm describing don't happen on their own. You can't create it by yourself, and the organization can't do it without you. Of the scores of lessons our team learned while conducting this research, the biggest insight of them all was:

Leaders animate culture.

You are that leader! You have the vision, trust, authority, opportunity, and responsibility. Only leaders can create and sustain a vibrant High Performance Culture.

Play this game well, and you will be astonished by what your organization can become. Get ready for the highest-stakes game you will ever play.

Culture rules!

GAME BASICS

BEFORE YOU PLAY

Trust me, you can't play the game if you don't know the rules. And if you don't know the rules, someone's bound to get hurt.
—**Alyson Nöel**

D o you enjoy games? My answer is . . . it depends. My family will tell you games of pure chance are not my jam. Games involving some strategy, however, are much more enjoyable for me.

Before I started working on this book, I don't think I had ever read the instructions for a game. It's not that I don't care about the rules—I just have others in my family who *really* enjoy knowing, understanding, and enforcing the rules. I've always left this responsibility to them. However, when we decided to use a game as our overarching metaphor for this book, the research team and I started reading game instructions—from CATAN (formerly known as The Settlers of Catan, which I have won only once) to Monopoly, to the rules of golf, and many more. I also received coaching and feedback from an expert on game design.

He helped me understand, at a basic level, how to create a magic circle and prepare the players for a good game experience.

Informed by this crash course, I have attempted to build a book structure that is both informative and engaging. Here we go . . .

GAME OBJECTIVE
The objective is to build a High Performance Culture.

To qualify as High Performance Culture, three conditions must exist:

- **Alignment:** The vast majority of people associated with the organization must voluntarily and wholeheartedly commit to the Aspirations of the enterprise (the more people who enroll, the stronger the culture will be).
- **Performance:** Every organization has its own metrics of success (performance). When leading in the not-for-profit sector, higher education, government, faith-based organizations, or the military, High Performance will be defined differently in each sphere.

    Regardless of your end goal, High Performance Cultures produce superior results over time. Without these tangible and sustained results, you may have created a *good* culture—a place where people like to work—but strong performance is a hallmark of the type of culture this book is dedicated to help you produce. Greatness hinges on execution and culture is the oil for the hinge.
- **Improvement:** There must be an ongoing effort to improve the culture. An organization clinging doggedly to

the past may shine brightly for a season, but it will not last. Is your culture getting better? Building a High Performance Culture requires constant vigilance and effort.

ABOUT THE GAME

The Game Objective includes the word "build"—and that is the intent and the goal. Some have suggested the best leaders can do nothing more than "shape" or "nudge" the culture in a particular direction. I believe they can do much more. Leaders are the architects of the future. But regardless of the verb you embrace, the game is afoot when you decide not to accept the status quo or the fragments of performance left behind by a previous leader. If you see a preferred future for your organization and sign up for this game, you will need to be a change maker; observers need not enter the fray.

To play the game well and apply the rules you'll learn momentarily, you need to understand a few basic truths about culture, regardless of the size of your organization, your industry, or geography.

Leaders animate culture. As I revealed in the introduction, this simple truth is the key to playing the game well. The word "animate" literally means "to bring to life." Leaders must embrace their unique role as the primary catalytic force required to ignite and sustain their culture—otherwise, the strategies and tactics that follow will be irrelevant. Too many leaders delegate the responsibility for culture. This is leadership malpractice. The work of creating culture must certainly be shared, and portions of it should be delegated, but leaders must never forget they are the champions of culture.

Culture is unseen but always present. Culture is an unseen force impacting everything that happens in an organization. It affects the thoughts, feelings, beliefs, decisions, and actions of every employee every day. The culture of your organization impacts who wants to join your team, who you select, how you write job descriptions, how you lead, how you are structured, who is recognized, who is rewarded, how agile your organization is, how innovative you are, how well you execute, and so much more. It is your water. But what comprises the water? What are its elemental components? Simply stated:

Culture is the cumulative effect of what people see, hear, experience, and believe.

Leaders need help building culture. Although senior leaders are the catalytic force in the creation of a High Performance Culture, they cannot build the culture alone. Leaders will need to enroll every other leader as an agent of the culture. And, ultimately, no culture is sustainable without the participation of the individual members of the group. Culture is an unseen force yet one that emanates from, and is sustained by, everyone in the organization.

Culture is typically built slowly. Because culture is the synthesis of what people see, hear, experience, and believe, its formation can span years or generations. Author and consultant Jim Collins uses the image of a flywheel to depict the ongoing effort required to create something as complex as organizational culture. The process resembles relentlessly pushing a giant and very heavy flywheel, turn upon turn, building momentum until a point of breakthrough and beyond. In Collins's analogy, there is no single turn, not even the last turn, that matters more than any of the others. The cumulative effect of *every* single push is what makes the difference.[1]

The flywheel effect is the typical way cultures are created. However, there are occasions when culture is shaped abruptly—one policy, one incident, or a single decision can quickly change a culture. A layoff, merger, product recall, scandal, or even dramatic success can have an immediate impact on the culture of an entire organization.

Culture is experienced individually. There is a real temptation to talk about culture collectively. After all, it is a shared experience. But culture is actually the combination of many individual encounters and perspectives. We must be careful when we paint with broad, sweeping strokes. This is why listening is such an essential skill if you want to become a master at culture craft. One data point from our research underscores this in vivid detail. When asked to what extent their organization is a great place to work, senior leaders and associates differ in their responses by almost forty percentage points worldwide.

Culture has roots in the past. If we are not careful, we can falsely assume the culture of any organization is merely a reflection of current practices and experiences. This view misses the influence of past leaders, former practices, and memories of previous circumstances. Even when these past experiences occurred outside your organization, such as toxic behaviors prevalent in an acquired company, environmental factors, disruptive technology in your industry, or changes in government regulations, they can still influence the way people see their current reality. Our challenge is to learn from the past but not live there. We would be naïve to assume the past is irrelevant. The wise leader will always leverage insights from the past while creating a better tomorrow.

Every culture is unique. No two cultures are alike; each has the fingerprints of the leaders who created it. Even though there are only three rules when it comes to culture, there are many more moves and infinite permutations available to animate your culture. The reason to mention this here is to encourage you to avoid the temptation to compare your culture to others and to be even more careful not to copy what you see is working somewhere else. Forgery is a crime. If you copy the practices of others, they probably won't work nearly as well at your organization. Create your own masterpiece.

Culture is shaped at two levels. As you probably already know, there are countless ways to shape and influence culture. When looked at broadly, these various levers and methods can be placed in one of two categories: structural or proximal. Structural influences are typically those that impact many people and are often reflected in systems and policies. Examples include compensation, benefits, and formal recognition and promotion criteria.

Proximal influences are much more localized and are often personal and individual. A supervisor who calls to offer condolences during a personal loss is a good illustration of this type of influence. While both of these forms contribute greatly to the culture of an organization, it is typically the proximal activities that have an outsized impact on an employee's perception of the culture.

Every culture can be enhanced. You may already know this, but not everyone does. I recently talked to a leader who was flabbergasted when I suggested the work of culture never ends. He really just wanted to "install" a better culture and be done with it. I shared with him how I have had the privilege to work in and on our organization's culture for over forty years. What you see today is not the product of last week's efforts; it is the accumulated effect of decades of work by hundreds of thousands of people. Regardless of how strong, aligned, and vibrant your culture is, you must keep working—your culture can always be stronger.

Leaders are the guardians of culture. Leaders must remain vigilant. I addressed earlier the fact that cultures are generally built slowly. Erosion is a slow process as well. Without careful attention, little things can eat away at a once strong culture. Sometimes the warnings will be obvious. Other times, they will be hidden in plain sight. In an ideal world, every member of a culture will be its defender, but the ultimate responsibility rests with its leaders.

TIME REQUIRED

In the instructions for virtually every game, you will find an estimate regarding how long it will take to play. I don't want to discourage you so early in our time together, but the truth is that you will *always* be a steward of culture. Everyone in a position of leadership is automatically registered as a player in this game. The only way out of the game is to quit or be removed from leadership.

As leaders, we have the opportunity and responsibility to engage and enhance the culture of our organizations on a moment-by-moment basis. The game of culture building never ends. If we play it well, we can leave the game with a sense of fulfillment regarding what happened on our watch. If we play poorly, we will leave the game with a sense of unfulfilled promise or, worse, regret. The culture you build, good or bad, will outlive your time at the table.

THE RULES OF THE GAME

The challenge our research team embraced was clear: How do you express in the simplest terms possible the irreducible minimum contribution a leader must make to create the culture their organization needs? In essence, what are the rules of the game? We knew we had to strive for simplicity without becoming simplistic.

This concept of forging clarity and simplicity in the midst of what is clearly a complex endeavor is not a new practice. One of my favorite examples is from the Navy SEALs.

In 2005, the SEALs were updating their ethos. Former SEAL Brent Gleeson describes the situation: "We had been moving at the speed of war for four years and eventually realized that we had never really defined (on paper) who we are, what we stand for and why we exist."[2] A part of the ethos they documented is the mantra "Shoot, Move, Communicate."

For me, there is something liberating in the clarity of these three simple words. Certainly these three actions do not encompass all the SEALS need to know or do, but from this foundation, they can engage and prevail. Their mantra breeds competence and confidence in the midst of the unknown and the chaotic. The stakes could not be higher for these warriors—lives, theirs and others, hang in the balance, and yet they move forward. Shoot, Move, Communicate.

This entire book is intended to give you a similar level of clarity, competence, and confidence in the face of your unknown future.

Just as the SEALs have succinctly captured the essence of

their battle plan, the following chapters will introduce you to the three simple rules you will need to master throughout your leadership career. Here's a quick look at what's ahead.

HIGH PERFORMANCE CULTURE

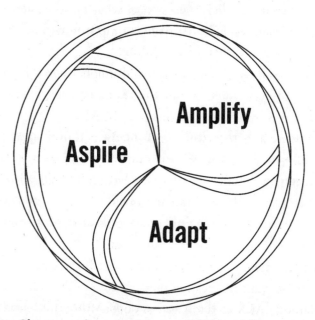

Aspire: *Share your hopes and dreams for the culture.*
Amplify: *Ensure the cultural Aspiration is reinforced continuously.*
Adapt: *Always work to enhance the culture.*

THE MOVES

As I mentioned earlier, culture is the cumulative effect of what people see, hear, experience, and believe. Therefore, as leaders, we have an infinite number of options at our disposal when we think about how we want to shape and build the culture of our organizations. Here's an example:

In the game of chess, each piece has predetermined movements by rule—the rook can move vertically and horizontally, the bishop moves only diagonally, and so on. However, despite their restricted mobility, these pieces can still make an infinite combination of moves in the hands of a grandmaster. The same is true in the game of culture building.

This vast array of options is one of the reasons it is so critical for us to be strategic in our thinking and disciplined in our actions.

There are only three rules, but there are infinite moves (Best Practices) you can make. We will devote the bulk of this book to sharing some of the moves that have worked well in other organizations. I share these moves not as a script to be followed but as a way to expand your thinking and stimulate your creativity.

YOUR MOVE...

Take another look at the three conditions that must be met to qualify as a High Performance Culture: Alignment, Performance, and Improvement. How is your organization doing in these areas?

WHY PLAY THE GAME?

Leadership is a stewardship.
It's temporary, and you're accountable.
—**Andy Stanley**

In games requiring more than chance, the right (good) moves are rewarded, and the wrong (bad) moves are punished. The same is true with culture craft. However, leaders have many competing priorities in the business world, and if you're not careful, the distractions of today can destroy your culture and your future. Organizations do not drift toward greatness.

If you want to simplify what's at stake and begin to understand the scale of your opportunity, I refer you to the great management and leadership thought leader Peter Drucker. He said, "Culture eats strategy for breakfast." He was right, but I want to do more than give you an insightful and pithy quote.

Let me start with something you already know: *every* organization has a culture. In some cases, the culture creates real, sustainable competitive advantage and superior levels of performance. In others, the culture is a source of significant organizational drag. Left unaddressed, your culture can produce more than drag; as the toxins increase, a culture can actually kill an organization.

For many of you, neither of these extremes reflects your current reality. So why would you want to consider playing the game? I'll share just a few reasons at this point—others will emerge in the pages that follow.

- Treading water is not an option. There are no stagnant cultures—each one is growing in strength and vitality or losing its essence, energy, and life force.
- A thriving culture will release the untapped potential in your people and your organization.
- If you are a person who likes to avoid risk, you should be interested in building a High Performance Culture because it is a hedge against irrelevance or worse. A healthy culture can prevent you from becoming the next Enron or Lehman Brothers.
- Finally, a High Performance Culture is the ultimate competitive advantage.

EARLY WARNING SIGNS

I want to make a brief case regarding why you, as the leader, should make culture one of your highest priorities. This section is brief because most leaders already understand the priority they should place on culture. No need to burn unnecessary word count to convince you of something you already know. Consider this a reminder.

First, I want you to think with me about some of the warning signs you have seen when toxins begin to invade a culture.

For those of you more analytically minded, hang on. We'll close this chapter with some hard data to support what I think we know intuitively—culture is a game too important not to play. If you sit this one out, you are jeopardizing more than just profits.

One more word about qualitative, or soft, data. I'll be the first to admit experience is a lousy teacher; only *evaluated* experience has the ability to change us. But assuming you will do the work of reflection and learning, we should not discount our experience or our intuition but instead treat these like additional "soft" data points.

I know virtually everyone has experienced unhealthy cultures. At a recent event, I asked a group to share with me signs that a culture might be struggling. Here are their thoughts, with a couple of mine thrown in for good measure.

- Turnover
- Absenteeism
- Low engagement
- Poor results
- Errors
- Theft
- No energy
- No fun
- Poor communications
- No passion
- Negative attitudes
- Denial
- Absence of joy
- Politics
- Waste
- Stagnation
- Unsafe environment
- Morale issues
- Mistrust

Note the group gave me the bulk of this list in about sixty seconds. My guess is if I had given them ten minutes, their list would probably have had a hundred items.

The point: we all know an unhealthy culture when we

experience one. The question is, what are its implications for the organization?

For now, I'll challenge you to figure that out for your organization. What would the benefits be if you eliminated the items on the list above? What if you just cut the list in half? The impact on sales, profits, customer satisfaction, engagement, share price, retention, market share, and more would probably propel you to the top of your industry. Food for thought, surely.

Now, for those who patiently waded through the "soft" section and are waiting for the "real" data, here you go.

THE DATA

When we began to explore the data supporting the case for culture, we looked first to our own research. We surveyed 6,063 women and men from ten countries. These people were divided into three groups: senior leaders, mid-level leaders, and frontline associates.

Here are a few of our findings. We'll share more throughout the book:

- Seventy-one percent of US leaders believe culture is their most powerful tool (67 percent globally).
- Sixty-eight percent of leaders around the world believe making culture a top priority is a requirement for positive business outcomes.

Secondary research also revealed a compelling case for culture:

- Thirty years ago, the impact of culture was already clear. A 1992 study spanning the previous eleven years found a

756 percent increase in net income in companies focused on culture compared to a 1 percent increase in those without performance-enhancing cultures.[1] If this study were conducted again today, I have no doubt the financial case for culture would be even more compelling.

- According to McKinsey's Organizational Health Index, companies with top-quartile cultures post a return to shareholders 60 percent higher than median companies and 200 percent higher than those in the bottom quartile.[2]

- In 2015, LSA Global studied 410 companies across eight different industries and found highly aligned companies (i.e., those with strong cultures) produced better financial results. LSA Global's definition of alignment included three different metrics: the firm's strategic clarity, a trustworthy and clear understanding of the culture, and high-performing talent. Based on the research, highly aligned companies achieved a 58 percent faster revenue growth and were also 72 percent more profitable when compared to unaligned companies.[3]

For some of you, the data is clear and the jury is in—creating a vibrant culture is good for business. True. However, some of the results you can anticipate transcend the financials.

As we will discuss in more detail in a later chapter, organizations around the world have chosen to use a wide variety of metrics to evaluate the vitality of their culture. This is good—you need to measure what matters to you. Here are a few other popular indicators of cultural health beyond the profit and loss statement and the balance sheet:

In 2016, according to Gallup, the pioneer of engagement metrics, more satisfied employees had 17 percent higher productivity, 70 percent fewer employee safety incidents, and 40 percent fewer quality incidents. Additionally, when compared with business units in the bottom quartile of engagement, those in the top quartile experienced 41 percent less absenteeism.[4]

Does high engagement equal a vibrant culture? We'll have this debate later. I do believe logic and experience indicate people who care more about their work, their co-workers, and their organization produce more. And if a workplace is toxic, high performance and outcomes like these are highly unlikely:

> According to McKinsey, companies more than ever need a purpose for workers to align on and contribute toward: "Seventy percent of the employees we surveyed said their sense of purpose is largely defined by work. Senior executives in our sample nudged the average upward, but even so, two-thirds of nonexecutive employees said work defines their purpose. This signals a clear opportunity for employers and leaders—an open door to encourage your employees at all levels to develop and live their purpose at work."[5]

However, the same study from McKinsey discovered a huge gap between senior leaders and others in organizations:

> Yet when we asked if people are living their purpose in their day-to-day work, the gap between executives and

others mushroomed. Whereas 85 percent of execs and upper management said they are living their purpose at work, only 15 percent of frontline managers and frontline employees agreed. Worse, nearly half of these employees *disagreed*, compared with just a smattering of executives and upper management.[6]

THE COST OF NOT PLAYING

The previous examples point to the upside of making culture a strategic priority. However, if we choose not to focus on culture, the downside is more than the absence of the results we just highlighted.

The world is changing. Digital natives are now entering the workforce—young people who grew up with technology as their constant companion. They walk into your organization with strong opinions. In many instances, they bring their own views of how an organization should be run, what success really looks like, and what they expect from their leaders. The best organizations are striving to understand and meet the needs of this younger workforce, many of whom value workplace culture and purpose over salary. Here is a stat that should get your attention:

> In a 2019 Glassdoor survey, 56 percent of workers ranked a strong workplace culture as more important than salary. This trend is even more pronounced among millennials and Gen Z. Leaders of all generations need to get a grip on this as the war for talent continues to intensify.[7]

We cannot afford to miss the future by doubling down on what has worked in the past.

A few years ago, I had a younger employee challenge me about providing him with an office. He said, "You are trying to reward me and my peers with the perks of your generation. Can I just have a large table out in the open so I can sit with the people I need to collaborate with on a regular basis?" This was a pre-pandemic conversation; today, I'm guessing that same employee would be asking why he can't work remotely and collaborate via Zoom. The world continues to change. Are you willing to change to keep up?

CULTURE BLINDNESS

One more potential reason to think deeply about culture: you and I may not have a good sense of what is really going on in our organization. Am I saying you are out of touch? Probably.

First, there is data that indicates how difficult it is for leaders to stay grounded in reality. And to make matters worse, this only gets harder the higher you rise in an organization. So, as it relates to culture, the senior leaders—arguably the most influential people in forming and sustaining the culture—are the farthest removed from the truth about their workplaces.

This phenomenon was revealed in stark relief during our global study. When we asked participants whether or not they would recommend their organization as a great place to work, 67 percent of leaders said yes, compared to only 27 percent of frontline associates who said the same. Although the numbers varied slightly by country, there was typically a thirty to forty percentage point gap between the two responses.

Do not be deceived by your own experience. You may have significant opportunities and results you are leaving on the table because you think everything (from a culture perspective) is great. By the way, wouldn't you want 100 percent of leaders and associates to say their organization is a great place to work? The only way to achieve this is to build and maintain a strong culture.

ENDGAME

Would you play a game you couldn't win? Before you are too quick to respond, what if the win was ongoing rather than confined to a single, game-ending move? The concept of an infinite game seems applicable here.

If you are not familiar with the premise, you may want to check out the work of James Carse from New York University. He wrote the classic text on this concept, titled *Finite and Infinite Games*. For a more recent take on Carse's work, you can read *The Infinite Game* by Simon Sinek. Here's a quick overview of the idea.

Some games have known players, clear boundaries, and a definitive end. At the end of the game, someone wins and someone loses. Examples of this type of game include chess, football, Monopoly, baseball, golf, tennis, *Super Mario Bros.*, and countless others. You play a finite game to win.

Infinite games, on the other hand, are played for an entirely different purpose. The goal, or win condition, is to continue playing, and for some, to continuously improve at playing the game. Relationships are an infinite game, as are parenting, personal fitness, and building your legacy. Many leaders would also consider business to be an infinite game. Building an enduring, great culture is also an infinite game. But why would you invest the energy?

Building a High Performance Culture is the infinite game that, when played well, sets you up to win the finite games of sales, profits, and customer satisfaction—just as weight training for an athlete is an infinite game that gives them the strength and energy to win their finite games.

As you consider the prospect of creating a High Performance Culture, I don't think you really want the game to end. Yes, your season at the table will end, hopefully of your own accord, but the game will go on. This is the way healthy, vibrant, aligned cultures work. The players and the leaders change, but the organizational "wins" are daily and ongoing . . . forever.

What is required of the leader? Just like the SEALs' "Shoot, Move, Communicate," you must consistently Aspire, Amplify, and Adapt.

If you are diligent in applying these rules, you will significantly increase your odds of creating a High Performance Culture. However, the goal is not just to be able to say you have such a culture. The ultimate goal: your culture becomes your primary competitive advantage and the driving force behind sustained levels of superior performance.

Finally, don't be surprised if you find the work of building a High Performance Culture personally gratifying. For many leaders, helping others identify with and invest themselves fully in the pursuit of a higher purpose will become the crowning achievement of their careers.

YOUR MOVE...

Make a short list of three to five things you believe would improve in your organization if you had a stronger culture.

Rule #1

ASPIRE

*Share your hopes and dreams
for the culture.*

A NEW GAME

In a world full of game players, the only way to
set yourself apart is to be a game changer.
—Matshona Dhliwayo

When Henry Ford started the Ford Motor Company in 1903, his organization was the tip of the spear for an industry that would literally change the world. Ford democratized the automobile. Lesser known are some of the innovations Ford introduced to make this possible.

Ford created the first moving assembly line, which reduced the time required to build a car from 12.5 hours to one hour and thirty-three minutes. To combat high turnover, Ford doubled wages to $5 per day and reduced the work week to five eight-hour days. This enabled his workers to earn enough to buy the car they were producing. He also offered profit sharing tied to production output.[1] These and other progressive ideas propelled the company past the 300,000-cars-per-year barrier in 1914. By 1920, Ford was producing more than one million cars per year.[2] The culture at Ford in those early days was built on the idea of efficiency.

Ford did excel at mass production. However, his focus on the customer was not as evident. You might say he had "producer logic," a term coined by Rosabeth Ross Kantar describing a deeply held belief that an organization knows better than its customers what they want and need.[3] Ford famously said customers could have any color Model T they wanted, as long as it was black. This statement was born from the fact that black paint dried more quickly than the other paint colors, thus reducing production time—another nod to his throughput bias.

Word War II was a challenging season for the company. Ford survived by playing a major role in the war effort, producing ambulances, aircraft, armored cars, and tanks.[4]

In the 1970s, Ford fell prey to the same competitive pressures plaguing the other members of the Big Three automakers. Gas prices were soaring, and foreign competition was on the rise. Japan was making higher-quality vehicles, and American consumers were taking notice.[5] The culture of producer logic, which had served the organization fairly well for half a century, was now totally outdated. Producing the most cars was no longer the prize the auto manufacturers were striving for. Environmental factors, competition, and changing customer expectations demanded a new cultural Aspiration.

As the American auto industry continued its slide, William Clay Ford Jr., the great-grandson of Henry Ford, decided a change in leadership was needed. In 2006, he recruited an unlikely savior.

To say Alan Mulally was a veteran of the aviation industry would be an understatement. As the CEO at Boeing, he worked on the 727, 737, 747, 757, 767, and 777 projects. When he joined Ford in 2006, many in the press and the industry felt he was the wrong man for the job. As the weeks and months following revealed, however, they were wrong.[6]

Mulally inherited an organization in disarray. They were hemorrhaging cash—in the year he arrived, the company was forecast to lose $18 billion. In addition to the Ford, Mercury, and Lincoln brands, the company had acquired Land Rover, Volvo, Jaguar, and Aston Martin. All of these other brands Alan would eventually divest. He would also close Mercury.[7]

The turnaround began with Mulally focusing on his team. He decided to keep the senior leaders he inherited—an act which confused many observers. He instituted a weekly business review. He felt it critical that the team confront reality and then work to course-correct where needed.

Each week, the global leaders would meet and share a status report on their critical projects and deliverables. Mulally wanted the entire team to know the status of their most important work. Were they on schedule? Did they have adequate resources allocated? Were they going to finish the work by the agreed-upon deadline? The answers to these and other questions were categorized using an elegant and simple coding process of red, yellow, and green. If a project was on track, it would be coded green. If it was just slightly off track, the situation would be labeled as yellow. If a project was significantly off track, a red designation would be used.

Mulally was initially taken aback by the reluctance of the leaders to admit there were any problems. The company was on track to lose $18 billion, and yet everyone at their first meeting said "green" on every project. According to them, they were all "on plan."

In response, Mulally said, "Well, we're all on plan, but we're losing billions of dollars. I guess our plan must be to lose billions of dollars! Let's try this again next week."

Weeks went by with lots of green on the scorecard—until, finally, somebody stood up and said, "Red—we are not on plan, and we don't have a strategy to get on plan."

Mulally stood up and applauded. He said, "You know you're not on plan, and you don't know how to get there. It's okay. Thank you for having the courage to say so."[8]

This was a turning point for the organization. It's always a good thing to have leaders willing to confront reality.

Mulally went on to clarify his Aspiration. He established One Ford—a purpose, a campaign, a strategy, and a plan to revitalize the company.[9]

Under the One Ford banner, Mulally sought to unify the organization as one team under one plan. He wanted the company to build quality cars equipped with the latest technology and provide these best-in-class cars at a price everyone could afford. His aim was to create a culture in which people were proud of their company's heritage and the future they were creating together.[10]

By 2010, Mulally had restored the organization, bringing its net income to $6.6 billion.[11] As he steered it safely away from the brink of bankruptcy, Ford's share price grew from $7.81 when he arrived to $17.72 when he retired in 2014.[12] Under Mulally's leadership and unifying vision, Ford was able to regain its place as an American icon.[13]

One of the lessons from the Ford story is that without careful, focused attention, great organizations can lose their way. Cultures, regardless of their strength, must be stewarded by their leaders, who must continually Adapt to maintain the vitality of the culture. We would all like to avoid the pain and trauma associated with "saving an organization" the way Mulally did.

Ford's miraculous revival began with Mulally's hopes and dreams for the organization and its culture. Leadership always begins with a picture of the future.

RULE #1: ASPIRE

What is the cultural Aspiration for your organization? This is the question Alan Mulally had to wrestle with at Ford . . . and so do you.

The first rule when building a High Performance Culture:

> **Aspire: Share your hopes and dreams**
> **for the culture.**

Every great culture begins with an Aspiration. Leaders call forth the best from themselves and those they lead. If you already have an Aspiration, is it clear, compelling, and pervasive? I am amazed by the number of leaders who have not given enough thought to the question of their Aspiration. Ambiguity on this single issue guarantees unwanted stress, strain, and unrealized expectations in the future. We interviewed many leaders who admitted this foundational rule had been violated in their organization. Each of these conversations reminded me of this famous conversation from Lewis Carroll's *Alice's Adventures in Wonderland*.

> **Alice:** "Would you tell me, please, which way I ought to
> go from here?"

> **The Cheshire Cat:** "That depends a good deal on where
>   you want to get to."
> **Alice:** "I don't much care where—"
> **The Cheshire Cat:** "Then it doesn't much matter which
>   way you go."[14]

Where is your organization going? Not just in terms of sales
and profits—what type of organization are you trying to build?
What do you want to be true about your culture?

In navigation, the star Polaris is also called the North Star
because of its position directly over the North Pole; it appears
to be stationary in the night sky, with all other stars revolving
around it. Therefore, it is a constant in the heavens. This constancy enables travelers to set their sights and sails toward it and
know they are moving true north. What is your cultural North
Star? Here's the fun part: you get to decide!

As with all three of the rules you will learn on the following pages, your answer for your organization is *your* answer. No
two organizations are alike. Therefore, you cannot—nor should
you—try to copy someone else's Aspiration. You don't want a
veneered replica of someone else's culture. You want your own.

Now, I will quickly say you may see qualities or characteristics in other organizations' cultures that you'll want to incorporate into your ethos. That's wise—as long as admiration doesn't
become blind adoption. We had a consultant years ago who challenged us to become "FedEx fast" and "Disney friendly," both
admirable traits. He was not saying we should *become* FedEx
or Disney. Any effort to clone or transplant their culture would
have been a disaster.

We will talk much more about this, but the blinding flash

of the obvious is: you cannot build what you cannot articulate. Nor can you create a sustainable, vibrant culture without a high degree of alignment.

When I say "high degree of alignment," I know this sets off alarm bells for some of you. You are concerned, rightly so, about the uniqueness, individuality, and diversity of people. To be crystal clear, alignment is not about sameness—it is about synergy.

What we see most often in an organizational context is addition: the work of individuals is simply added together to equal the output of the group. This is a very low bar for performance.

Synergy is about multiplication. Rather than merely adding together the output of individuals, working together can create an almost magical multiplication effect. The work of the group exceeds the cumulative input of the individual members. Synergy should be the goal of every organization. Alignment is the path to synergy.

The best organizations across the globe have a growing sense of the power resident in their people. There is also an increasing awareness of the value for the enterprise when people bring their whole selves to work. Alignment is about harnessing the individual brilliance, passion, and talents of everyone and channeling them toward a common cause. What is the cause? The shared cultural Aspiration.

Leaders who ignore or violate this first rule do so at high risk to their influence, their longevity, and the performance of the organization.

WORDS MATTER

A word about terminology before we go any further. Ford's turnaround story under Mulally's leadership was certainly impressive.

A key to Mulally's success was his commitment to a new shared language at Ford. Do you have a shared language in your organization? Does your entire workforce have clarity on your Aspiration and the words you will use to describe it? Just because something is clear to you does not mean there is clarity in the minds of your organization.

Over the years, the questions I have received most often around the concept of a shared Aspiration revolve around terminology.

- What is the difference between vision and mission?
- What's the difference between purpose and vision?
- Should we have a vision, purpose, and mission?
- Does every organization have an ethos?
- Do I have to use any of these words to build a great organization?

How do we simplify all of this? I'm fearful my answer is not going to satisfy you any more than it has the countless leaders with whom I've shared it previously: you get to decide!

Are you a leader who craves detail? If so, we can parse out the difference between these terms (we'll help you do this later in the book). Or are you a leader who thrives on a minimalist view and loves simplicity? In either case, you can design a solution tailored to your preferences.

Here's the big idea on this topic. All of these terms—vision, mission, purpose, ethos, and values—are different ways to do one thing: to help you crystalize, clarify, and articulate the Aspiration you have for your organization. If you or your organization desire a high level of precision and will not be overwhelmed by the complexity of it all, you can use all of these mechanisms to help people understand the Aspiration. Each one can represent a different facet of your hopes and dreams.

We will explore each of these (ethos, vision, mission, etc.) in greater detail in upcoming chapters. Once you decide which term or terms you will use, then comes the most critical part of the process:

> ## You must define the word(s) you have chosen for your entire organization.

It really doesn't matter which terms you use, as long as your organization knows how you define them. As one example, a leader of a large nonprofit organization told me "mission" is their word for why they exist, not "purpose"—fantastic! As long as there is alignment within *your* organization.

If you do not define the terms for your organization, confusion will rule, not culture. Confusion creates organizational drag; clarity accelerates progress.

Only when there is clarity about the meaning of the word(s) being used can you then effectively communicate your *specific* Aspiration. You cannot align on the culture you are trying to create if people don't understand the words you are using. Shared language is one of the cornerstones of all High Performance Cultures. Do yourself a favor and take the simple step to establish a common vocabulary. Words matter!

YOUR MOVE...

What are your hopes and dreams for your culture? If you don't know or aren't totally confident in the way you have presented your thoughts to your organization, keep reading.

USE THE FORCE

A problem well defined is a problem half solved.
—**John Dewey**

E thos is the fundamental character or spirit of a culture, the underlying sentiment that informs the beliefs, customs, or practices of a group or society.[1]

The best leaders understand their opportunity to create, sustain, and unleash the spirit of a culture. This is no small task, nor one to be taken lightly. As evidenced in the Ford story, ethos is pervasive and unseen, life-giving or toxic.

Think about organizations you have been a part of during your career. What was the spirit of their cultures? I know you have an answer, and your response probably came to mind quickly. Your memory of a given culture may be positive or not, but the ethos is clear.

Here's another question: Do you believe the ethos you remember was the product of conscious effort on the part of leadership? Were the leaders of the organization trying to create what you experienced? In far too many situations, ethos just is—it exists but is not thoughtfully crafted, curated, and cared for.

Tragically, in most situations, if the ethos is organic and left to develop untended, it ultimately becomes toxic.

The first thing you must do if you want to create a High Performance Culture is decide what you want the ethos to be. You don't have to call it ethos; most don't. What you call it is irrelevant. What matters is that you have a clear, compelling picture of the culture you are trying to create. In this chapter, we will explore a couple of ways some organizations articulate their desired ethos. In subsequent chapters, we'll look at several other tools, including vision, mission, purpose, values, and more. All of these are mechanisms and tools at your disposal to help your entire organization understand the type of culture you want to create. As John Dewey reminds us, "A problem well defined is a problem half solved."

FREEDOM AND RESPONSIBILITY

In 1997, Reed Hastings and Marc Randolph were looking for an idea to scale. This had been the topic of their daily carpool for some time. One day, they hit upon the idea of distributing movies by mail. What made this feasible was the advent of what was then cutting-edge technology: DVDs. These discs were small and sturdy. They could be mailed in a simple envelope at a very low cost. From this simple idea, Netflix was born. What happened next is a case study on building a global powerhouse using unconventional thinking and methods.[2]

Hastings began Netflix with many of the leadership and management paradigms he brought with him from prior work experiences in Silicon Valley, but to his credit, he was open to new ideas. What quickly formed was a desire for a different type of workplace, a different culture—one he described as being known for "freedom and responsibility."[3]

Hastings was an outlier. Many startups and small organizations fail to recognize the importance of culture. At Netflix, the fact that early senior leaders made conscious, strategic decisions about the culture they wanted and the type they did not want is an exemplar for other organizations. Don't wait until you're big to pay attention to culture. Your lack of attention at an earlier stage in your life cycle could be the sole reason you don't become a big company. Healthy cultures enable healthy growth.

Although I am not aware of Hastings nor any member of his team ever using the word "ethos" when describing their vision for Netflix, this is still the perfect example. A clear, concise, and compelling way to describe what they would devote themselves to creating. Over the years following Netflix's origin, hundreds, if not thousands, of leadership decisions and countless employee decisions would be driven not by rules but by ethos.

To help employees and potential employees understand its ethos, Netflix published its Culture Deck. This 125-slide presentation goes into great depth explaining what the company believes, what they are trying to create, and the behaviors that lead to an employee's success with the organization. The original 2009 version is still available on the internet (as is the current version). As of this writing, the deck has over 21 million views.[4]

Here are some of the things Netflix says and does to foster its ethos of freedom and responsibility:

Adequate performance gets a generous severance. The

first principle Reed built Netflix on is the idea of talent density. If the people are amazing, you need fewer of them. These are the people who create a great place to work. However, for this to happen, you need a team of "A-level" performers. Thus, this first practice was born.

Hard work is not relevant. Because the culture is built for performance, Reed and his team would say how hard you work or how many hours are required for you to complete your work is not a valid point of conversation. The more pertinent question: How are your results?

Increase talent density faster than the growth of complexity. Netflix is quick to acknowledge the growing complexity in the world. It also knows most organizations' response is to add more people—but this is not Netflix's plan. Netflix has chosen to increase the caliber and capability of its staff. By doing so, it can mitigate the impact of growing complexity rather than compound it with more headcount.

We are a team, not a family. Teams that win consistently field the best talent, move people as needed, and cut people if they cannot perform.

Pay top of market. This is one of the keys to maintaining talent density. Think of this like a team without a salary cap—the market determines the value of each player. This mechanism also helps attract and retain the best. Many organizations try to minimize their labor expense, but not Netflix.

Provide context, not control. This is a key lever in fostering the ethos of freedom and responsibility. One of the primary roles for all leaders at Netflix is to provide enough context to enable people to make their own informed decisions.

No vacation policy or tracking. If you want to scream

freedom and responsibility from the rooftops, you can. Or you can tell people to take vacation as they see fit and continue to produce great work.

I am not suggesting you adopt *any* of the practices I just outlined. These specific tactics only work if you are in the right industry and attempting to build a culture of freedom and responsibility. What I can say is this: culture is a big deal at Netflix.

During our research for this project, we had the opportunity to speak to a Netflix leader. He was thriving and excited to be part of the team. I asked him, "How often do you talk about the culture?" After a brief and quizzical look, he said, "Every day . . . many times every day." As if this comment were not enough, he went on to say all the other leaders he knows in the company talk about the culture every day, too. How often do you talk about your culture?

What I hope you will be in awe of is the sobering level of clarity around the Aspiration at Netflix—an ethos of freedom and responsibility—and how it impacts so many systems, processes, and decisions the organization makes on a daily basis.

Despite their culture, Netflix is still part of a larger economy and subject to market and competitive dynamics like any other organization. Will their culture stand the test of time? How will they need to adapt in a changing world? These are questions every leader must answer.

JUST FOUR WORDS

Not all examples of a powerful ethos are confined to global brands. The power of understanding and embracing your

Aspiration is universally applicable in organizations of all sizes. The following examples are from more modest-sized companies.

While conducting interviews for this project, I met with a leader, Bob, who had a long-standing reputation for amazing and consistent levels of high performance in a multimillion-dollar service business. We sat down to talk about culture, and I learned his secret.

After patiently listening to me idle on about purpose, mission, values, and other drivers of culture, he said, "I like to keep things simple." Something in me knew whatever he was about to say would be noteworthy.

"Around here, it's all about trust, intensity, growth, and fun."

My response was something like, "Are those your values?"

"No," he said. "I don't really have values. Like I said, I want to keep things simple."

"So how do trust, intensity, growth, and fun help you?" I asked.

"They are *everything*. They're virtually all I talk about."

"How often do you talk about them?"

"Every day—and so do all my leaders. And if you ask my employees what it's like to work here, they're going to say something about trust, growth, intensity, and fun, too. I like to keep things simple."

Wow! The clarity was refreshing. Do you know the ethos you are trying to create? Can you represent it in four words? There's nothing magical about the number four, but four is better than ten—because as the number of attributes you are trying to instill and nurture increases, the harder your job will be. If not a few words, is there a phrase, an image, or maybe a metaphor that represents your desired ethos?

THE LIGHTHOUSE

How much do you know about lighthouses? Honestly, my knowledge on the topic is quite limited. However, I was inspired to learn more when I met a leader who chose the lighthouse as the symbol representing the ethos he wanted to create in his retail business.

In the beginning, before selecting the lighthouse as his preferred metaphor, there was clarity regarding his aspiration. This leader knew he wanted to "be a blessing to his guests like no other place of business." Yet, he wasn't sure how to convey this message in a clear, simple, memorable, and compelling way.

Lighthouses are typically considered a warning beacon for ships approaching treacherous waters—but this is only one of their functions. Another responsibility is to help weary travelers find their way to a safe harbor. A lighthouse is a sign of welcome as much as a sign of warning.

While preparing to host a dinner for his new employees, their families, and invited guests to launch his new business, he said he was trying to figure out two things at once: how to convey his vision and how to decorate the tables. It was a eureka moment! "We want to be a light that shines brightly and draws people in," he said. "Let's use lighthouses for the table centerpieces."

To remind his team of their Aspiration, he has given each a small lapel pin of a lighthouse. They wear the pins both as a reminder and a conversation starter. Often, a customer will ask about the pin, opening the door for the employee to share the company's Aspiration—its ethos.

Almost twenty years have passed since that dinner, and his team's light still shines brightly in his community. The ethos is clear to all, on both sides of the counter.

WHERE DO YOU BEGIN?

The thought of articulating the ethos of your organization may be thrilling or daunting. Regardless, I want to give you some steps you can take. This is work you can share, but you cannot delegate it away. The ethos should be a reflection of your head and your heart.

Here is an activity to help you begin this important work.

Step One: If you were going to list ten words to characterize your organization at some point in the future, which ten words would you select?

Step Two: Cut the list in half—you can only keep five. Rank them in order of priority.

Step Three: Scratch numbers four and five. What do you think about the remaining three words?

Step Four: Write a paragraph for each of the three words, describing in vivid detail how each one will be manifested in your ideal future. Each paragraph should be no longer than 150 words. Then edit or rewrite the paragraphs as necessary to end with a single sentence describing each attribute of your ethos. For bonus points, pick just one of the three. What would happen if this single word represented your ethos?

OR, YOU COULD ASK...

If you lead an existing team, department, division, or organization, design a simple survey with one question:

How would you describe our culture?

Leave the word count open on the survey. If someone wants to write a word, a sentence, a paragraph, or a white paper, let them.

When you receive the input, put all the responses in any software program capable of creating a word cloud and see what you learn. You may discover your ethos is well established. Perhaps it even aligns with your Aspiration. If so, congratulations! If not, you will have a better understanding of the scope and scale of your task ahead.

———

To recap, the first move you must make if you want a High Performance Culture is to decide and declare what you are trying to create. What is the spirit, the essence, the ethos of your ideal culture? You can use any language you want to describe this or use no label at all. Like Bob, maybe you just want to keep things simple.

YOUR MOVE...

Assume for a moment you could create your dream organization. Which three or four words would you use to describe its ethos?

LEAVE NO DOUBT

The two most important days in life are the day
you are born and the day you find out why.
—Mark Twain

S ome organizations have never articulated their "official"
ethos, yet their sense of destiny is rock-solid and their cultural Aspiration is unwavering. Many of these organizations find power and energy in a clearly articulated purpose. In
this chapter, we'll look at several cases to demonstrate the central role purpose could play as the cornerstone of your cultural
Aspiration.

In a parade of never-ending unknowns, a clearly articulated
purpose will leave no doubt in the hearts and minds of your
entire organization as to why it exists. For many people, purpose
provides an emotional and intellectual anchor. An organization's
purpose can change, but it is typically the most steadfast of all
the terms used to articulate the Aspiration. This stability is often born of an unshakable resolve in an unchanging motivation.
Goals, strategies, and tactics evolve, but purpose is generally held
as a constant.

PERFORMANCE WITH PURPOSE

PepsiCo is known in every country on earth, but this was not always the case. From humble beginnings in 1919, this global brand thrived during the Great Depression by undercutting the competition, selling its Pepsi drinks for five cents.

In the mid-sixties, PepsiCo began a shift into the packaged goods arena when it acquired Frito-Lay.[1] In 2005, PepsiCo overtook Coca-Cola in market value,[2] but even with this victory under its belt, PepsiCo leaders knew change was coming.

By this time, there was a confluence of several global trends reshaping the world. Most notable for the food industry was a much higher concern with health and wellness. This was combined with the explosion of social media and a growing global consciousness around corporate social responsibility, including environmental stewardship, fair trade, sustainability, water rights, waste management, working conditions around the world, and more.

Indra Nooyi, a former Boston Consulting Group consultant and senior leader at Motorola, joined Pepsi in 1994 as the senior vice president of strategic planning. Within a year of joining, one of her first projects was the restructuring of the organization.[3] In the years that followed, she moved to finance. Then, in 2006, Nooyi was named CEO.

Upon assuming her new responsibilities, she quickly acknowledged the shifting environment and wanted to position the company well in the changing landscape of the future. Although profits at the company had doubled during her early tenure, largely due to shrewd strategy and wise acquisitions, she knew the organization needed a fundamentally different direction. Her response: the Performance with Purpose (PwP) program.[4]

One of the challenges with such succinct proclamations is the likelihood some will interpret the Aspiration as just another attempt at sloganeering—the craft of creating catchy taglines. The ability to find the perfect words to convey an idea is actually a handy skill. The problem arises when leaders employ this talent and think their work is done. For a purpose or any slogan to serve an organization well, there must be substance, not just sizzle. Fortunately for PepsiCo, Nooyi knew this.

She launched the four PwP pillars to provide the additional clarity the organization needed to move toward the new Aspiration.[5]

Financial Sustainability: Delivering superior financial results in a sustainable fashion with all stakeholders in mind.

Human Sustainability: Transforming the product portfolio by reducing the sugar, salt, and fat in their products while dialing up more nutritious foods and beverages.

Environmental Sustainability: Limiting the environmental impact by conserving water and reducing the company's carbon footprint and plastic waste.

Talent Sustainability: Supporting the company's women, families, and communities in new ways.

You may look at Nooyi's Four Pillars and think these are merely strategies. Call them what you will—strategies, strategic bets, big moves, focus areas, strategic priorities, or anything else you like. The point: if leaders really want to Aspire, they must do more than create a slogan or catchy phrase. The Aspiration has to have enough substance to provide direction and allow for critical evaluation along the way. Nooyi's Four Pillars brought PwP to life for PepsiCo.

THE RESULTS

Here are some of Nooyi's own words to describe the impact of PepsiCo's new Aspiration.

> PwP was my primary focus, and PepsiCo made tremendous progress. Our portfolio of more-healthful options grew from about 38 percent of revenue in 2006 to roughly 50 percent in 2017. We reduced water use in our operations by 25 percent from 2006 to 2018 and provided safe drinking water to 22 million citizens in the communities we served. We almost tripled our investments in R&D to expand our nutritious offerings and minimize our environmental impact. Women held 39 percent of senior management roles by 2018. After PwP was implemented, net revenue grew by 80 percent, and PepsiCo stock outperformed both the Consumer Staples Select Sector Index and the S&P 500.[6]

THE NEW AMERICAN UNIVERSITY

We started this section with a big example; yes, PepsiCo is a huge global enterprise. This should validate the scalability of the concepts we are exploring. However, the power of clear and compelling purpose can be seen in organizations of all sizes.

Higher education is not known as a hotbed for innovation.

With roots stretching back centuries, universities are one of the last bastions of the old world. Generally speaking, their pedagogy hasn't changed much in many decades, yet the cost of a four-year degree has increased 144 percent over the past twenty years for private institutions, and 211 percent for in-state public ones. As a result, colleges and universities across America are struggling.[7]

With soaring prices, limited access, and outdated methods, many are questioning the future of higher education. Are these institutions slowly losing their value proposition? Now, this is not to suggest top universities will not continue to provide a vital service to their students and the world. What is less clear is what will happen to the majority of schools—will they adapt, cope, or disappear?

Between 2016 and 2021, seventy-nine institutions closed their doors for good, merged, or stated their intention to do one of these things.[8] Many are suggesting the current model no longer works. Despite it all, most schools are slow to change.

What creates such a fierce reluctance to innovate, and what fuels the tendency to cling to the often-failing practices of the past? Probably too many factors to address here. However, there is another way to think about higher education.

When Michael Crow became Arizona State University (ASU)'s president, he set out to widen access to higher education. His actions were driven by the belief that universities were no longer fulfilling their social obligation to provide higher education to the next generation. One problem, as Crow saw it, was the increasing number of institutions that wanted to make their schools more selective and increase tuition, which limited access. Crow's "New American University" model has helped ASU become one of the largest public universities in the US.[9]

The purpose for the university, now found at the beginning of its charter, is this:

> ASU is a comprehensive public research university, measured not by whom it excludes, but by whom it includes and how they succeed.[10]

Part of this statement sounds like those of many other higher-learning institutions, but hidden in plain sight is something astonishing. To be measured "by whom we include and how they succeed" is both revolutionary and clarifying for the faculty and staff. This statement implies a radical approach to higher education.

Rather than focus solely on the transfer of knowledge to a limited number of people, ASU's success metrics include the size of the audience it serves and the success of its students. This is a classic shift from producer logic to customer logic. In essence, ASU has said, "We are here to serve you and enable your success . . . oh, and by the way, we want to do this for the masses, not a select few."

To fulfill this groundbreaking purpose, innovation is a necessity. ASU's online education wing now brings in $150 million every year in revenue. The school is also forming partnerships with the business community. ASU and Starbucks are providing access to online degrees for thousands of Starbucks baristas. This type of innovation is a strong signaling mechanism to the seriousness of the organization and, from a pragmatic side, helps close the gap created by the continuing cost pressures referenced previously.

While the state of Arizona has slashed funding for its public universities and colleges, ASU has increased its enrollment by more than 50 percent under Crow's tenure. Today, enrollment is above 135,000, including more than 57,000 in online degree programs.[11]

Crow said, "Innovation is infused in ASU's DNA because we are designed to spark, support and manifest new ideas. Innovation can be found at all levels of our education, our research and our community engagement. It drives our perpetual evolution and it will continue to guide us as we work toward solutions to the next great challenges of a complex future."[12] In 2020, ASU was named the most innovative American university for the sixth year in a row.[13]

I suggest that ASU's unconventional purpose has created an unconventional ethos. Crow and his team are bucking the historical norms. They have created an institution built on innovation and driven by purpose.

THE CRADLE

When our team's plans were finalized to travel to the Pinehurst Resort in Pinehurst, North Carolina, I have to confess: I wasn't totally focused on the fact that we were going to interview Tom Pashley, its president, for this project. Honestly, I was thinking more about the opportunity to play at one of the most storied golf courses in the world. The golf resort, the largest in North America, is comprised of nine courses and all the amenities you would expect. But for me, it is not the scale that sets Pinehurst apart, nor the amazing level of hospitality, but the tradition.

Pinehurst was founded in 1895, before golf was well known in the United States. At that point, the game was not new to the rest of the world; historical references to the game appear in numerous ancient texts, and the "modern" game emerged in St. Andrews, Scotland, in the 1400s. The first written record can be found in 1457, when James II banned the game because it was viewed as an unwelcome distraction to people learning archery.

Donald Ross made his way to America from Scotland, arriving with only $2 in his pocket. The fact that he had apprenticed under Old Tom Morris at St. Andrews Golf Club made it easier for the young Ross to land a job. He was hired to design the first four courses at Pinehurst and eventually became the head professional on staff.

Since those early days, Pinehurst has hosted US Opens both for men and for women, Ryder Cup matches, PGA Championships, US Amateur events, and many more.

Imagine the complexity of stewarding an organization with more than a hundred years of influence and more than a thousand employees. Pashley and his team understand their opportunity and their responsibility.

During our meeting with Pashley, he talked about the process they had been through as they affirmed and clarified their purpose and values. He shared candidly the painstaking and, at times, arduous process their leaders had navigated.

Pashley said some of their meetings felt as though they were going in circles. Then he showed us a small wooden model of a spiral staircase. What he and his team realized from time to time during the process was that they *were* actually going in circles. They likened their experience to walking up a spiral staircase, and with each revolution, they gained altitude. The higher they climbed, the better their perspective. This new perspective led them to new levels of clarity on the purpose of their grand old organization. Here is what Pashley shared:

> As the cradle of American golf, we honor timeless traditions and inspire legendary stories, one smile, one round, one moment at a time.

Over the next few days on property, I had the chance to play several rounds of golf, make a few memories of my own, and receive countless smiles from Pashley's team. The experience made me think the entire staff knew the script. I would say they were well grounded in their purpose thanks to the work of Pashley and his leaders.

———

Some leaders bristle at the idea of purpose. You may be one of those leaders. I've talked to many of you over the years. If I had to summarize what I've heard, I would say you think the concept is, well . . . soft. You are more comfortable with hard assets, hard numbers, and more tangible things. I understand. But there is something magical about clarity of purpose. (I realize referencing purpose as magical probably does nothing to debunk your sentiment regarding the softness of the concept.)

What does magic have to do with organizational health and high performance? Everything. Everything, that is, if you consider channeling and releasing the human spirit relevant. People want to be well led. How do you lead well without telling people what you are trying to accomplish and why it is important? All of the leaders we have profiled in this chapter understand purpose can provide a clarion call that brings out the best in people.

WHAT IS YOUR PURPOSE?

Before you determine your purpose, you need to consider if having a stated purpose would help your organization. My personal bias is yes, it would. However, what is *more* important is for your organization to have a clear Aspiration. You may choose to represent this in other forms—mission, ethos, values, or some combination of these.

If you do decide a purpose statement is part of your arsenal for establishing the cultural Aspiration, here are a few questions that may help.

The first is: Why does your organization exist?

This is no trivial question, and it's one many leaders have wrestled with and come out with totally different and very unique conclusions.

> **Coca-Cola Company:** Refresh the world. Make a difference.[14]
>
> **Johnson & Johnson:** We believe our first responsibility is to the patients, doctors and nurses, to mothers and fathers and all others who use our products and services.[15]
>
> **Netflix:** To entertain the world.[16]
>
> **Ferrari:** To make unique sports cars that represent the finest in Italian design and craftsmanship, both on the track and on the road.[17]

Now, let me ask you again: Why does your organization exist? The essence of purpose is it always answers the question "Why?" Your purpose can offer specific strategies and tactics;

however, this is a slippery slope. By definition, strategies and tactics change with circumstances. In an ideal world, I would argue that a purpose should be much more steadfast. The stability and predictability of your purpose give the organization confidence in a changing world.

Just a few more questions for now...

- What was your organization born to do?
- What fires you up about the future you are trying to create?
- What is it about the future you envision that compels you to pursue it?
- What do you want the legacy of your organization to be one hundred years from now?
- How would you explain *why* you exist (not what you do) to a small child?
- What greater good can your organization contribute to the world?
- If your organization went away, what would the world lose?

All of these questions are intended to stimulate your imagination and help you cut through the fog so you can answer one fundamental question: *Why* does your organization exist? The answer to this question is your purpose.

YOUR MOVE...

Why does your organization exist, really?

DREAM BIG DREAMS

*Dream no small dreams for they have no power
to stir the hearts of men.*
—Johann Wolfgang von Goethe

Have you ever started on a trip without knowing where you were going? Maybe, but I doubt it.

Perhaps as a young person, you said, "We are going to drive across the country," and began your adventure without a specific plan or itinerary. However, even with such a broadly stated intention, it still informed your decisions. If you wanted to drive across the country and were starting in San Diego, you didn't go south into Mexico. If you knew you wanted to drive, you didn't need to go to the airport. You probably knew your general sense of timing and pace—were you planning to take a year or a month to cross the country? You likely knew how much you would invest—were you planning to sleep in your car or find five-star hotels? Even loosely defined objectives and predetermined notions can provide a degree of clarity for cross-country trips, just as they can for organizations.

One of the mysteries I imagine I will never fully solve is why so many leaders do not tell their organization where they are trying to go, what they are trying to accomplish, or what they are attempting to become. I do have a few theories regarding their silence.

The leader doesn't know. Seeing the unseen is extremely difficult and requires a blend of foresight, courage, optimism, and time. Many leaders have not invested the time to formulate their own vision of the future. This lack of clarity can be paralyzing for a leader and an organization. You cannot share what you do not know.

The leader doesn't believe. The essence of leadership is creating a better tomorrow, envisioning a preferred future, and rallying people to make it a reality. The catalytic character trait needed to pull this off is an internal locus of control. The leader must believe in their ability to affect outcomes in the future. If the leader believes success or failure is out of their control, they will always be timid when discussing the future.

The leader doesn't know how. This is a fundamentally different challenge from the previous two. In this case, the leader probably has a fairly good idea of the future they would like to create. The root problem is they do not know *how* the organization will get there. I would suggest that this is very common. Even the best leaders rarely know the exact "how" when they declare the "where." Charting the course to the preferred future is most often the work of the organization.

The leader fears failure. Fear makes cowards of us all. Leaders often fail—sometimes in small things, sometimes in big things. But leaders try. Leadership is rarely about certainty. All we can be certain about are our intentions and the level of effort we will expend. There are any number of historical quips and quotes that might be appropriate here. I'll just conclude this point with a well-known excerpt from Theodore Roosevelt.

> It is not the critic who counts; not the man who points out how the strong man stumbles or where the doer of deeds could have done them better. The credit belongs to the man who is actually in the arena, whose face is marred by dust and sweat and blood; who strives valiantly; who errs, who comes short again and again, because there is no effort without error and shortcoming; but who does actually strive to do the deeds; who knows great enthusiasms, the great devotions; who spends himself in a worthy cause; who at the best knows in the end the triumph of high achievement, and who at the worst, if he fails, at least fails while daring greatly, so that his place shall never be with those cold and timid souls who neither know victory nor defeat.[1]

The leader is not leading. A final potential cause for a leader to not tell the organization where they are trying to go or what they are trying to become: the leader is not leading at all. This does not mean they cannot lead; it just means in the present situation, they are not providing leadership. Let's face it: not everyone in a position of leadership is leading.

Leadership is about helping people move to a preferred future. If you are not doing this, perhaps you are managing or trying to protect and control, but you are not leading. Systems, processes, and assets need to be managed; people need to be led. Not declaring a destination or Aspiration makes perfect sense if you are not attempting to lead.

Leaders working to build a High Performance Culture must overcome all these barriers and others.

Assuming you are bold enough to see the unseen and declare it for others to see, how do you state your intentions? How do you make your Aspiration approachable for others? How do you make your preferred picture of the future tangible—to the extent that something that doesn't yet exist can be tangible—to those you hope to rally? These are nontrivial questions.

We've already reviewed two of your options—ethos and purpose. In this chapter, I'll give you two more mechanisms to consider: vision and mission. Although many use these terms interchangeably, I want to help you see them as two different tools at your disposal. They can be used independently or in tandem.

VISION: THE BIG PICTURE

Vision is a broad and directional picture of the future. Of the different mechanisms for articulating the Aspiration, vision statements are the most likely to inspire and encourage people. Unfortunately, many vision statements are too technical and precise to inspire. In many cases, they also try to say too much. A great vision statement captures the essence of your Aspiration, not the details.

As you read the following statements, you will undoubtedly see the similarities between some of these and the statements you just read representing purpose. This is the slippery slope I mentioned previously. There is no consensus in the leadership literature on common definitions for these terms. A lot of really smart people define and use these terms very differently. That is okay. In the end, you, as the leader, must pick the term or terms you want to use and how you will define those words in your context.

In many organizations, vision is their source of inspiration and meaning. Here are a few vision statements that fit this definition. You can decide for yourself how inspiring they are.

IKEA: "To create a better everyday life for the many people."[2]

Whole Foods Market: To nourish people and the planet.[3]

Amazon: To be Earth's most customer-centric company.[4]

CVS: To help people live longer, healthier, happier lives.[5]

Habitat for Humanity: A world where everyone has a decent place to live.[6]

Fight the urge to be too specific and detailed in your vision—unless specificity is required based on the type of organization you are leading. I assume engineers, for example, would be more inspired by specifics because that is the world they live in. But for most people, inspiration and clarity do not require all the details.

Some would say Dr. Martin Luther King Jr.'s "I Have a Dream" speech was a great example of vision. He did not say, "I have a strategic plan" and then proceed to unpack the specific details when he stood on the steps of the Lincoln Memorial in 1963. Rather, he said:

So even though we face the difficulties of today and to-morrow, I still have a dream. It is a dream deeply rooted in the American dream. I have a dream that one day this nation will rise up and live out the true meaning of its creed: "We hold these truths to be self-evident, that all men are created equal."

I have a dream that one day on the red hills of Georgia, the sons of former slaves and the sons of former slave owners will be able to sit down together at the table of brotherhood.

I have a dream that one day even the state of Mississippi, a state sweltering with the heat of injustice, sweltering with the heat of oppression, will be transformed into an oasis of freedom and justice.

I have a dream that my four little children will one day live in a nation where they will not be judged by the color of their skin but by the content of their character.

I have a dream today![7]

YOUR VISION

What is your dream for your organization? What is your vision? Where do you look for it? In your head and your heart. Here are some questions that will help you discover your vision for your organization.

- What are you convinced that your organization should endlessly and tirelessly strive for?
- What is big enough that you could work toward it your entire career and then pass the baton to others to pursue?
- What is so big and so admirable, you can think of nothing better to devote your leadership energy toward accomplishing?
- What would catapult your organization into the future?
- What pursuit would energize you and your people?
- What is something you feel must be passionately pursued?

Think over the horizon. Think about your life's work. Think about your contribution to the world. Think about your legacy as a leader. Think big, and then think bigger. Johann Wolfgang von Goethe's words on this topic are a personal challenge for me: "Dream no small dreams for they have no power to stir the hearts of men."

MISSION: THE NEXT MOUNTAIN TO CLIMB

The word "mission" is often used to articulate a long-term (typically, five to seven years) goal or Aspiration. More short-term objectives are typically referred to merely as "goals." However, by definition, a well-crafted mission *is* a goal—just usually bigger and with a longer time horizon.

"Mission" is a word with rich meaning and potentially profound implications. The denotation includes "being sent to complete a specific task." Leaders establish the task to be accomplished and commission the people to pursue it.

Whether the mission is military, corporate, organizational, or even personal, the task must be explicit and concrete. A mission can be labeled successful or not depending on whether the specific task was completed.

Therefore, the best mission statements are specific, measurable, and time-bound. You would not typically work on a mission forever. As we established earlier, the forever-type Aspiration is probably better defined as a vision or purpose. Let's take a deeper look at the quintessential example of a mission from President John F. Kennedy.

On May 25, 1961, the president stood before Congress and said America should "commit itself to achieving the goal [mission], before this decade is out, of landing a man on the moon and returning him safely to Earth."

He checked all the boxes with this single statement. The mission was long-term in nature but still time-bound: "before this decade is out." The task was specific and well defined: "landing a man on the moon and returning him safely to Earth." These first two attributes together also made the mission measurable—the entire world would know if the mission was a success or not.

Kennedy gets bonus points because the mission was also bold and inspiring. Here are a few excerpts from what he said in a speech on September 12, 1962.

> Those who came before us made certain that this country rode the first waves of the industrial revolutions, the first waves of modern invention, and the first wave of nuclear power, and this generation does not intend to founder in the backwash of the coming age of space. We mean to be a part of it—we mean to lead it. For the eyes of the world now look into space, to the moon and to the planets beyond, and we have vowed that we shall not see it governed by a hostile flag of conquest, but by a banner of freedom and peace. We have vowed that we shall not see space filled with weapons of mass destruction, but with instruments of knowledge and understanding.
>
> Yet the vows of this nation can only be fulfilled if we in this nation are first, and, therefore, we intend to be first. In short, our leadership in science and in industry, our hopes for peace and security, our obligations to ourselves as well as others, all require us to make this effort, to solve these mysteries, to solve them for the good of

all men, and to become the world's leading space-faring nation.

... We choose to go to the moon in this decade and do the other things, not because they are easy, but because they are hard, because that goal will serve to organize and measure the best of our energies and skills, because that challenge is one that we are willing to accept, one we are unwilling to postpone, and one which we intend to win, and the others, too.

... And, therefore, as we set sail we ask God's blessing on the most hazardous and dangerous and greatest adventure on which man has ever embarked.[8]

Anybody want to go to the moon? There is a reason Kennedy's words are used decades later to illustrate the power of a well-conceived and well-articulated mission; this speech was one of his finest hours and a model for leaders who want to lead a team, organization, or nation to accomplish the unimaginable.

The United States did successfully accomplish the mission on July 20, 1969 (before the end of the decade), when Neil Armstrong became the first man to walk on the moon.

If you use this approach, it is important to establish another mission once you have completed the current one or when you find your people searching again for meaning. This was one of the lessons learned from NASA's Apollo program. There was no compelling mission after the moon landing. History tells us that tens of thousands of the world's brightest minds left NASA to find another "moonshot" (aka mission).

Now, back to Earth—could a mission help you articulate

your Aspiration? Perhaps. Here are a few questions to help you sort through this.

- What advantages would you anticipate if your entire organization had its version of a "moonshot?"
- What could you strive for in the mid-term future that, if achieved, would have a multiplier effect in your organization?
- What goal could you establish to create a positive ripple effect on your entire organization (perhaps requiring unprecedented levels of collaboration and cooperation)?
- What goal is so big from today's perspective that you might deem it impossible? Note that when Kennedy established the moon mission, the required technology did not exist.
- To what extent would your organization be energized by a really bold and challenging long-term goal?
- What could you do to make your mission compelling and inspiring?

Depending on how you answered these questions, you may want to use a mission statement to clarify and articulate your Aspiration. If not, no worries; you have other tools at your disposal.

A CAUTIONARY TALE

As previously mentioned, I have worked at the same company for almost forty-five years. My tenure has been marked by several different roles and even a few career changes within the business. I started in our warehouse and mail room, and I also had the opportunity to start a few departments: Corporate Communications, Quality & Customer Satisfaction, and others. I've worked in Restaurant Operations, led our Training & Development group, and more. I have had a very full and fulfilling career. That's the nice way to say it, anyway. I was once introduced by a colleague as a guy who couldn't hold down a job! There is some truth in his comment.

I remember one specific transition to a new team that taught me a lot. The president of the company accompanied me to the first meeting with my new department. I knew this was not really to introduce me; he was there to show his support. I was glad he had my back. After I was introduced, one of the team members asked me about my vision for the department.

I don't know if this question would have surprised you or not. You could easily think, *Seriously, I am brand new—this is my first day. How could I have a vision?*

Well, I was not surprised by the question, and if you are leading, I don't care if it is your first day or your thousandth—people expect leaders to have a vision, even if they don't use that exact word.

Here's what I said: "I see this team having more influence, more impact, and more reach in the future..."

Before I could even finish my thought, the team member interrupted me and said, "No, no, that's not what I am talking about."

"What are you referring to?" I asked.

"I want to know if the work I do is going to continue. Who is going to be my supervisor, and where will I sit?"

"I don't know any of those things," I said. "But here's what I do know: we are going to have more influence, more impact, and more reach. We will work together in the weeks and months to come to answer your specific questions."

Here's the point: people generally want certainty, but rarely can you and I provide that certainty. Dr. King didn't have certainty; President Kennedy didn't know all the answers regarding how we would accomplish the moon mission. Certainty is almost always just out of our reach. However, what we *can* provide is clarity.

This first rule is about Aspiration, not absolutes. The only certainty we can provide as we look to the future is intent and effort; we cannot guarantee the outcome.

YOUR MOVE...

How might having a stated vision or mission serve your organization?

LEAD WITH VALUES

In matters of style, swim with the current.
In matters of principle, stand like a rock.
—Thomas Jefferson

What drives behavior? This is a huge question, and the answer is obviously multifaceted. However, one of the key drivers is what we believe about the world in which we live and work. As we consider our behaviors in the workplace, countless organizations use values to influence how people think (that is, what they value) in hopes of impacting their day-to-day behavior.

I will begin this chapter with a confession: I have been a fan of core values for a long time. When we began this project, I worked diligently to manage my own bias, but here we are. As we compiled our research, it quickly became clear that I could not talk about articulating one's cultural Aspiration without discussing values. I am more convinced than ever that the right values, clearly stated and deployed well, are one of the most powerful culture-shaping tools leaders have at their disposal.

When an organization states its values, it is setting

expectations and boundaries regarding how people think and work. In essence, leadership is saying, "This is what we believe. This is who we strive to become. This is how we work around here."

In some organizations, values have been repositioned to make them more personal. If you pursue this route, you may choose to position your values as "cultural commitments" or "common commitments." This is another case where the language you choose is up to you. Just be clear and consistent. Values, by any name, can clarify and codify what is important in your culture. Well deployed, values are unifying.

VALUES CREATE TENSION

Yes, values, once articulated and activated, can unify an organization. But on many occasions, they will also create tension; most Aspirations do. When a clear picture of the future exists—stated as vision, mission, purpose, values, or whatever mechanism you choose—the gap between your current reality and your Aspiration will be highlighted. This is good tension! The leader then has the opportunity to rally the organization to close the gap.

There is another type of tension that can arise when values are stated clearly: the gap between stated and operational values. Stated values are what you say. Operational values are what you do. Let me illustrate.

If your organization professes to care deeply about safety, yet you allow hazardous working conditions to persist unchecked, there is a gap between stated and operational values. This creates tension.

If one of your values is candor, yet no one in recent memory has been willing to confront reality, instead retreating to half-truths and dishonesty masquerading as niceness, this creates tension.

When we live and lead in a fashion inconsistent with our stated values, this creates tension.

If either of these types of gaps exists in your organization, don't be discouraged. Instead, work to close them. If you want your organization to be more innovative, call people to innovate. As an employee, if you believe the expectation exists for you to innovate, the odds of you doing so go up drastically. If you believe excellence will be honored, you might do one more review of your PowerPoint deck to check for typos.

Deployed wisely and referenced constantly, values can be an active filter for *how we think about our work*, and as a result, they impact *how we do our work*. The right values, reinforced through word and deed, impact our mindset and our behaviors.

VALUES ADD VALUE

When an employee joins your organization, I assume they want to be successful. I have met very few people during my career who didn't want to be successful. One of the strategies many people employ on their success journey is to do good work in a fashion that will please the boss.

One of the implications of this approach is that the new employee—and all employees, for that matter—will try to figure out what is important to the boss. Acting on this knowledge, combined with having a good work ethic, is a fairly legitimate way to advance in an organization.

However, if the leader doesn't tell this new person what is

important, they will have to guess. The fundamental problem is they may guess incorrectly.

So, another benefit of having core values: there is no more mystery regarding what behaviors, attitudes, and mindsets leadership values.

In addition to clarifying what the leaders and organization value, values can also:

- Help you know who to recruit and select
- Accelerate onboarding and training new employees
- Serve as the cornerstone for coaching conversations
- Anchor performance evaluations
- Provide meaningful points for recognition
- Help you identify future leaders

Every one of these applications helps you create an aligned High Performance Culture.

FORGOTTEN VALUES?

As I confessed in the opening of this chapter, I have been a fan of shared core values for decades, and perhaps you have been, too. However, even if this is true, there are still a few things you need to know (or be reminded of).

Having stated organizational values is not enough. Today, about 80 percent of large companies have published values. This fact alone is not particularly helpful. All it tells us is that a lot of companies have adopted this relatively new business tool by taking the first step of documenting a set of values. What this statistic fails to address is the efficacy of the values being published.

Many employees question the relevance of their organization's values in the day-to-day business.

- A mere 27 percent of US employees strongly believe in their organization's values.[1]
- Only 23 percent of US employees feel confident that they can apply their organization's values to their work every day.[2]

I have yet to find a statistic that reveals how many employees even *know* their organization's values. I would guess the number would be extremely low.

Here's another challenge for you to watch out for.

I was with a group of leaders a few years ago that wanted to change their organization's core values. I began to probe. As far as I could tell, there was nothing fundamentally wrong with their existing core values. There had been no significant strategic shift, senior leadership had not changed, and there was no new vision. I couldn't figure out what was up, so I asked why they felt the need to change the values. What they told me was revealing. "These core values are not working."

You can guess what they meant by this statement. My assumption was that the organization was not receiving any perceived benefit from their current values.

My response was simple: values never work unless leaders do.

Leaders must constantly share, reinforce, and celebrate their values, as well as challenge those who fail to uphold them. I am not aware of any organization that can merely articulate their values and *poof*—the values are immediately embraced, recruiting materials change, selection criteria changes, recognition programs miraculously morph to align with the new values, and so on. Leaders determine the value and impact of core values in an organization.

The sad ending to this story is that the leaders I spoke to did change their values, and now, just a few years later, the new values aren't working any better than the old ones did. The problem wasn't the values.

GOOD VALUES?

If you do a Google search for "core values," you will find examples such as:

- Integrity
- Boldness
- Honesty
- Trust
- Accountability
- Passion
- Fun
- Humility
- Continuous learning
- Ownership
- Improvement
- Leadership
- Diversity
- Innovation
- Quality
- Teamwork
- Simplicity
- Employee development
- Discipline
- Empowerment
- Authenticity
- Commitment to customers

Here's the potential problem with this list: most of these descriptors could apply to any organization. Also, several of these are character traits. Let's examine these two issues independently.

Differentiate with values. What is it about the way your people think or work that differentiates you? If you select empowerment, improvement, and diversity as your core values, how do they set you apart from millions of other organizations? If you include only generic terms to define your Aspiration, it may not be worth the effort. Values should add value, not describe something obvious or articulate attributes that should be table stakes.

Will your list of core values be *totally* unique? Probably not. However, it should help your employees understand what is different about your approach to the work. The more your values can differentiate you from your competition, the more value they will add.

Select for character. If you include character traits as core values, you miss a huge opportunity—you actually forfeit the power of having values in the first place. Calling out honesty, integrity, and trustworthiness as your core values is suspect. Every organization should be able to select people who possess basic and fundamental character traits. Use your values to say more and do more—with some effort, they may even enable you to articulate your competitive advantage.

NAME THE THING

I have been asked many times if it is okay to include Aspirational values on your list of core values. I think all values are Aspirational—some just may require more work to become a reality than others. It is always helpful to name the thing you want to become. Be prepared: some will push back. For instance, "How can we say one of our values is creativity when we are not creative?" A value is never fully inculcated. Every person, every day, should strive to make the thing real to the fullest extent possible. Values are an ongoing and daily pursuit.

If you do include values that are clearly and perhaps fully Aspirational, the trick is in communications. Don't try to convince your organization that it's something it's not. However, if you have attributes in mind that you hope will *become* core to who you are as an organization, be sure to tell everyone the truth. Cast a compelling vision for why these values *must* become a reality.

Please don't miss what's most important here—whether values are currently reflected in your organization or are purely a vision of your preferred future state, they must align with and support your overall Aspiration for the organization.

LEARN FROM OTHERS

If you have yet to codify your core values or feel that your current values need a refresh, you may find it helpful to see some examples from other organizations. I am not endorsing the following values nor suggesting you should copy them. Remember, your values must be your own. However, I think we can learn a lot from others.

As you read the following examples, ask yourself a few questions:

- Would these values influence my thinking and my actions?
- Would these values help our organization excel in our chosen marketplace?
- Which of these values would help us articulate what is distinctive about the way we think and work?
- Are these values to instill, or are they character traits we should select for?

Starbucks

A global coffee company founded in Seattle in 1971, Starbucks now operates in eighty countries and employs over 380,000 partners. Global sales in 2021 were over $29 billion.

> With our partners, our coffee and our customers at our core, we live these values:
>
> - Creating a culture of warmth and belonging, where everyone is welcome.
> - Delivering our very best in all we do, holding ourselves accountable for results.
> - Acting with courage, challenging the status quo and finding new ways to grow our company and each other.
> - Being present, connecting with transparency, dignity and respect.
> - We are performance driven, through the lens of humanity.[3]

Royal DSM

Royal DSM is a global company in health, nutrition, and bioscience, applying science to improve the health of people, animals, and the Earth. It manufactures specialty ingredients for the food industry: yeast extracts, food enzymes, and much more. When the leaders decided to refresh their business strategy, they wanted a complementary set of values to drive the new behaviors. Given their multinational presence and few native-English-speaking employees, their values needed to be simple, easy to translate, and memorable. After a lot of work, Royal DSM leaders landed on:[4]

- Caring
- Collaborative
- Courageous

HubSpot

HubSpot is a software company specializing in inbound marketing, sales, and customer service. Founded in 2006, the company consistently ranks as a best place to work and is touted for its culture. Its values center on being:[5]

Humble
Empathetic
Adaptable
Remarkable
Transparent

Headspace

Headspace is a mobile application specializing in meditation and mindfulness. Through science-backed meditation and mindfulness tools, Headspace seeks to help customers around the world create life-changing habits to support their mental health and pursue a happier and healthier self. Headspace has three core values.[6]

- **Selfless Drive:** We accelerate each other and are accountable to each other to deliver on our vision.
- **Courageous Heart:** We bravely go to new places knowing we have the support of our team.
- **Curious Mind:** We learn that when we listen to others, we cultivate the curiosity and empathy to unlock innovation.

FROM MY WORLD

I'll close this section with a personal example. I have had the privilege to be a part of and lead many fantastic teams over the years. Here are the values from one of them. I share this to illustrate that sometimes the uniqueness of a word or phrase is in how you define it.

- **Radical Collaboration:** Our collaboration will not be a consequence of convenience or happenstance; it will be the product of a conscious decision and disciplined actions required to leverage our individual strengths.
- **Courageous Curiosity:** Our efforts to create and add more value will be fueled by our willingness to play the role of the explorer. We will ask the hard questions, pursue the unknown, and never stop learning.
- **Strategic Creativity:** Our creative thinking will be focused and purposeful. We are not interested in change for change's sake. Creative thinking may pave the way to a preferred future, but it is not the destination.
- **Breakthrough Results:** Incremental improvement is not our goal. We will prioritize, plan, and work to help the organization achieve extraordinary results. We will think big and act with conviction and boldness.

YOUR NEXT STEP

Your next step is to decide if you want to use values to shape the culture of your organization. I know some great leaders who don't, and you certainly don't have to. However, if you do, here are a few tips to conclude this chapter.

Simple and clear language. Clarity is your friend and a gift that you, as the leader, can give to the organization. The values are intended to inform, not impress. You probably want to express your values using language that requires little explanation. As an example, "innovation" as a value is fairly clear. However, "do good" leaves a lot of room for interpretation and questions. I will add that I think provocative and descriptive language is also a good thing—it can conjure up vivid images, which can help convey the underlying intent of the value (e.g., "customer obsessed" is stronger than "we value customers"; "radical collaboration" is stronger than "collaboration").

Distinctive (typically) trumps generic. Are there unique attributes of your organization you want to leverage or enhance (e.g., scrappy, courageous, audacious)? If so, these could be candidate values. I am not suggesting that excellence or innovation be removed from your list of values. Perhaps if you are manufacturing critical medical implants or if you are a design firm, these could make perfect sense. However, virtually every organization in the world could include excellence and innovation on their list of desired values.

Fewer is better. The more core values you have, the greater the likelihood that they won't add value. I don't think there is a magic number, but from my experience, the "right" answer is closer to five than ten. One of the benefits of having a shorter list is that you increase the likelihood of people actually using the values as a point of reference when making day-to-day decisions.

Stay the course. If you get the values right, they should stand the test of time. I am not suggesting that they will never change. Some of the reasons for changing them have already been mentioned—new leadership with a new Aspiration, new strategy, new behaviors needed to meet the demands of a changing world, and so on. However, if your values change too often, you will confuse your people and slow your progress toward your Aspiration. There is also a good chance you'll hurt your credibility and undermine your leadership.

What you don't want to happen is for people to say (or think), "This too will pass." If people don't believe that the values are going to stick, they may assume a passive or indifferent posture toward them. If this happens, you will undermine the Aspiration and make it even more difficult to build the culture you want. Strategies and tactics change frequently—values should be much more durable.

———

At this point, you know why you should strive to build a High Performance Culture and the critical importance of crystallizing and sharing your Aspiration. But, even if this was an epiphany, you cannot stop now . . . your work is not done. Let's move to the second rule and learn more about how to Amplify your Aspiration!

YOUR MOVE . . .

If you could create a list of three to five purely Aspirational values for your organization, which values would you choose?

Rule #2

AMPLIFY

*Ensure the cultural Aspiration
is reinforced continuously.*

HIT REFRESH

Our industry does not respect tradition—
it only respects innovation.
—Satya Nadella

n late 1974, Paul Allen had a hunch—an idea he thought might change the world. He had just picked up a copy of the January 1975 issue of *Popular Electronics*, featuring the Altair 8800, the first microcomputer, on the cover. He believed there was an opportunity to create software for the new machine. He shared his thinking with his high school friend Bill Gates, who was attending Harvard at the time. Just months later, Gates dropped out of Harvard, and the two friends started Microsoft.[1]

In the 1980s, some laughed at Gates's bold vision for the future of technology in the world. Yet, despite the naysayers and skeptics, his early dreams soon became a reality. Gates's focus on technology and innovation, combined with his business instincts, was a recipe for success. He helped the organization grow from the first year's revenue in 1976 of $16,005 to over $1 billion in sales in 1990.[2] During the coming decade, 90 percent of the personal computers in the world would be using their software.[3]

On January 13, 2000, Steve Ballmer succeeded Bill Gates and became the CEO of Microsoft. The next fourteen years were a mixed bag, to say the least. Ballmer always had a sales bias, and this predisposition allowed the company to triple sales and double profits on his watch. However, the stock price stagnated. Under Ballmer's leadership, the company's profit increase (16.4 percent) outpaced Jack Welch's at General Electric (11.4 percent) and Lou Gerstner's at IBM (2 percent).[4] However, despite these numbers, many believed that Ballmer was leading the company nowhere. By doubling down on its core products, Microsoft, people feared, would miss the future. In 2013, the BBC rated Ballmer as one of the worst CEOs.[5]

The problems with Microsoft during this era were not rooted in profitability. The issues were deeper—they were cultural. Without Gates at the helm, the culture changed significantly. People did not innovate; risk-taking was a relic of their storied past, and the future, they believed, would be an extension of the present. The success on the quarterly statements was a mirage. These numbers did not accurately represent the future of the company, although they did capture the essence of the culture.

Have you ever experienced anything like this? The apparent success Ballmer created was fool's gold. I don't know Ballmer, but it appears as though he had a transactional view of the business rather than a transformational one. He was no doubt a maximizer at heart; his actions reveal a desire to squeeze all the profit he could from the business. There's surely nothing wrong with a profit motivation, unless you are a CEO who fails to combine your maximizer tendencies with an awareness of a changing world and the possibilities of tomorrow.

The temptation to live in the past is real. When sales and

profits are good and even growing, leaders must be on guard. As Marshall Goldsmith so eloquently proclaims, "What got you here won't get you there."

By 2014, Microsoft had only 3.5 percent of the mobile market and 3 percent of the tablet market, and Azure, its cloud service, had been late to market, allowing Amazon to gain a huge share.[6] To top it off, Microsoft had no significant response to iTunes, and Google Chrome eventually surpassed Internet Explorer. The future was literally passing it by. After several failed acquisitions, languishing stock prices, and growing media pressure, Ballmer stepped down.[7]

Unfortunately for Ballmer, the future demanded new leadership—someone who could see past this quarter's profit and loss statement. On February 4, 2014, Satya Nadella succeeded Ballmer as CEO.

NADELLA'S ASPIRATION

Nadella joined Microsoft in 1992, while Gates was still at the helm. He had witnessed firsthand the changes in the culture under Ballmer's leadership. He knew he needed to "Hit Refresh," the name of his 2017 book, in which he chronicles Microsoft's efforts to rediscover itself. Gates himself described Nadella's challenge in the book's foreword, saying, "Satya has charted a course for making the most of the opportunities created by technology while also facing up to the hard questions."[8]

After a deep dive and extended period of listening to the people and reviewing the data, Nadella was able to confirm his suspicions regarding the culture. He described the situation as a loss of "fluidity, hunger, and energy associated with Bill Gates."

Nadella also named some of the specific challenges he would address. "Innovation was being replaced by bureaucracy. Teamwork was being replaced by internal politics. We were falling behind."[9]

In 2015, Nadella revealed Microsoft's refreshed mission: "To empower every person and every organization on the planet to achieve more." He noted that Microsoft would need a "dynamic learning culture" to make this a reality. From that point forward, the concept of a growth mindset—the idea that not only *can* every individual change, learn, and grow, but they also *must*—was at the heart of Microsoft's transformation.

Nadella didn't stop there. He wanted the new vision to be as clear as possible. When describing Microsoft's culture, he said the company would shift from being "know-it-alls" to being "learn-it-alls."[10]

SYSTEMS REFRESH

With the new direction established, Nadella and his team began to Amplify the Aspiration. In addition to a refreshed mission and renewed clarity about how the organization would work, systemic changes would also be made to support the new direction.

Screen People In ... Not Out
Microsoft created a significant cultural shift by thinking differently about employee selection. The team moved from screening people out to screening them in. Rather than focusing on what disqualifies a candidate, Microsoft is now much more interested in what unique qualities or attributes a person may possess that would add value to the organization. This change has created a more inclusive and diverse workforce.

Here is how Kathleen Hogan, Microsoft's chief people officer, describes this new approach: "At its core, Screening In reflects our desire to bring in talented people who aren't carbon copies of existing employees, because building a homogenous workforce isn't the best way to innovate and problem solve for the increasingly diverse customers we serve."[11]

This new philosophy prompted Microsoft to expand its recruiting efforts. Previously, Microsoft focused its recruiting on only a few universities. Today, the company recruits top talent from more than five hundred universities.

Hogan continues, "The idea is to find common ground with candidates, instead of ways of ruling them out. We want to make the interview process more tailored to the individual, and have interviewers approach candidates with a mindset of, 'How can I help them be successful here?' and, 'What skills and experiences do they have that we need?' and, 'Do they share our passion for our company's mission?' The intent is not to trip candidates up or find what's wrong, but rather find what's right and determine if we can succeed together."[12]

Performance Management

In order to align with the new Aspiration, systems and processes in the performance management domain also changed. As an example, the practice of employees "stack-ranking" one another was discontinued.

For those not familiar with the concept, stack-ranking involves ranking all employees based on performance and then taking corrective action on the bottom tier. Employees in this tier would either face immediate dismissal or be given "personal improvement plans."

Although you will find some leaders who promote this practice, the downside typically outweighs any advantage. Unintended consequences can include a decrease in collaboration, an erosion of trust, unhealthy levels of internal competition, and more.

Compensation systems were also modified. To Amplify the organization's commitment to the concept of a growth mindset, a significant portion of executive compensation is now tied to this key metric.

KEEP LISTENING

Now, almost a decade into his tenure, Nadella and his team know that complacency kills, and in striving to be true to the ethos of their new culture, they willingly embrace and continue to model a growth mindset.

At the heart of their strategy is a robust people-analytics team. At the time of our interview with a senior leader at Microsoft, the company employed seventy people in this function. Clearly, the company is committed to listening intently to its employees.

People analytics is a discipline that uses data to help leaders make better people decisions, as well as other types. Typically, at the heart of this function's responsibility is keeping a finger on the pulse of the organization. Using a variety of methods, this team listens to the entire workforce and synthesizes the information it mines from its efforts. In addition to these activities, people analytics can assist with several other business-critical roles.

Process transformation. A people analytics team in a global firm discovered a team that was producing a particular deliverable 16 percent more efficiently than its counterparts in other countries. Once this was determined, best practices could be mined and shared with other teams around the globe.[13]

Strategic change initiatives. By monitoring resource allocation and usage, timing, turnover, cycle time, engagement, and more, the people analytics team can provide a dashboard for senior leaders to assess the rate of change and its implications. This early-warning system helps guard against a failure due to "too much, too fast."

Workforce planning. In addition to the more traditional role of listening, a robust people analytics team can help you create the future. How many people will be needed to execute your plans? What skills will they need? What should be outsourced? What, if anything, should be phased out over time? How will the structure need to change to support future strategic initiatives? What treasure is hiding in plain sight within your organization? Probably more than you think.

FRONTLINE OPPORTUNITY

What does it look like in the real world to Adapt based on insights gained from intentional listening? We discovered a wonderful example at Microsoft. We learned that through its investment in people analytics, the company discovered an opportunity with its frontline leadership—shift leaders, team leaders, supervisors, and others who provide day-to-day leadership for individual contributors.

The senior leaders at Microsoft understood their role in the cultural transformation they were seeking. They also knew the limits of their influence. They understood that to truly transform their culture and help every employee—almost 200,000 of them—embrace a growth mindset, they would need to enroll existing frontline leaders differently.

> No one leader, no one group, and no one CEO would be the hero of Microsoft's renewal. If there was to be a renewal, it would take all of us and all parts of each of us.
> —*Hit Refresh* by Satya Nadella

One of the patterns I have seen throughout my career is the importance of frontline leaders. In countless situations, these are the people who make or break your change efforts. I remember vividly an encounter I had with the leadership team in a struggling organization. The team's level of clarity was refreshing and, honestly, a little confusing.

The senior leaders were totally aligned regarding the cultural changes they wished to make. They also sensed a readiness from the hourly associates. The problem: frontline leaders.

Frontline leaders are generally the least tenured, lowest paid, least experienced, and least skilled leaders on the payroll. The senior leaders I talked with acknowledged all of this, and yet they also acknowledged that these ill-prepared leaders were the linchpin between their Aspiration of a preferred future and reality. The most puzzling part of the conversation was that they had no plan or intention to address the situation.

What's your plan to enroll and equip your frontline leaders to help you create the culture you want?

Microsoft understood the critical role of its frontline leaders and the influence they had on its culture. To bring clarity to the job and the expectations, the leadership set out to hear from thousands of employees—it conducted interviews, focus groups, and surveys specifically targeted to learn about the efficacy and future role of its frontline leaders.

The conclusion was elegant in its simplicity. Every leader would be expected to Model, Coach, and Care.

- Model a growth mindset and the values of the organization.
- Coach people on how to be successful in their role.
- Care about people as individuals.

This level of clarity took the proximal influence of frontline leaders to new levels. Today, the training to accompany this focused job description has been deployed to their eighteen thousand leaders across the globe.

THE RESULTS ... THUS FAR

Nadella is not finished "refreshing" Microsoft, yet the results are impressive. There are many other things he and his team are doing to Amplify their Aspiration. The company's portfolio of products and services has become much more future focused and aligned with the changing world. Its market share in the cloud and in other areas is growing rapidly. According to *Inc.* magazine in 2021, 78 percent of the five hundred largest companies in the world use Microsoft's cloud services.[14] No longer is the industry ignoring Microsoft. Nadella has awakened the giant.

Not only have the products and services changed, but the culture of Microsoft has also changed. As Nadella might say, his global team has moved from being "know-it-alls" to "learn-it-alls."

As he predicted, this has been a very beneficial cultural shift. Not only have the employees noticed, but the world has as well. Since Nadella hit refresh on the culture, Microsoft's share price has skyrocketed from $31 in 2014 to $338 today.[15] As of this writing, Microsoft is battling Apple for the distinction of being the most valuable company on the planet.

RULE #2: AMPLIFY

As important as Nadella's Aspiration was for Microsoft, it was not enough. Aspiration alone will never create a High Performance Culture. The second rule provides the energy to transform what was previously only a dream into reality.

> Amplify: Ensure the cultural Aspiration is reinforced continuously.

In organizations around the world, many people are inundated by the demands of their lives and jobs. The contributing factors vary from person to person, but some of the typical ingredients are a grim blend of busyness, complexity, distractions, success, failures, fatigue, fear, and uncertainty. In my book *Smart Leadership*, I called this toxic mix "quicksand."

Regardless of the elemental components or relative toxicity, there is a high probability that many of the people in your organization are battling their own quicksand. If we don't extricate ourselves and help others do the same, we'll find no joy in our work, our productivity and our influence will be diminished, and our chances of building a High Performance Culture will be slim. However, this is not a book on how to escape the quagmire. If that is your challenge, read *Smart Leadership*.

So, why do I mention this here? Not to sell my book. I bring this up because you are leading in a world of quicksand. Even if you have managed to escape—and I hope you have—I'm guessing many of the people in your organization have not. Therefore, as the cultural architect, the one with a vison and an Aspiration, you must be aware of the context in which you are attempting to lead. The context demands that you Amplify your Aspiration, or else your dream will never be heard, much less realized, by your organization.

Why the word "Amplify"? Our team spent many hours debating the best word to describe this rule. In the end, we loved the literal denotation of the word "Amplify."[16]

1. To expand [the Aspiration] by the use of detail or illustration
2. To make larger or greater (as in amount, importance, or intensity)
3. To increase the strength or amount of

This is what the leader must do to ensure the Aspiration is heard and acted upon above the noise and quicksand of our daily lives.

The process of Amplification is demanding and multifaceted. We will address several moves in later chapters that may be helpful as you chart your unique course. However, just to be clear on the types of activities, systems, and levers that leaders can employ, here is a partial list.

Modeling	Recognition
Compensation	Vision casting
Selection	Rituals
Storytelling	Onboarding
Decision-making	Structure
Rewards	Symbols

The final thought I want to leave you with as you begin to think about how to Amplify your Aspiration is strategic repetition. Many of the items above should be utilized countless times in a given week—not just by you, but by all the leaders in your organization.

If you are the senior leader, you cannot delegate your responsibility for the culture, neither can you fulfill your role alone. You will need to share the Aspiration over and over again in countless situations, using a variety of methods, in order to break through the noise of the world and begin to embed your message in the hearts of your people. A message not heard consistently is a message without impact.

YOUR MOVE...

If Nadella himself took over your current role, what do you think he would do, and why?

FOLLOW THE LEADER

*Example is not the main thing in
influencing others. It is the only thing.*
—**Albert Schweitzer**

As you can imagine, there are countless ways a leader can Amplify the cultural Aspiration they have established for their organization. We will explore several of these later in this book. However, when our team began to debate which of these moves we would highlight and in what order, the contents of this chapter leapt to the top of my list, no question.

Leaders can say all the right things, and many do, but they can still fail miserably in creating the culture they say they want. Often, the primary stumbling block is the leader. People always watch the leader.

If you and I want to Amplify an Aspiration, the most powerful thing we can do is be a living, breathing example of the preferred future we hope to create. Our words and deeds carry disproportionate weight. Leaders throughout history have understood and leveraged this truth. You can, too.

THE WARRIOR KING

Alexander the Great was born the son of a king, schooled by the greatest minds of his day, and conquered the known world before he was thirty years old. Nearly 2,400 years have passed since he ruled, yet his influence still reverberates through history. Some consider Greece the cradle of modern Western culture. It was the fountainhead for such ideas as democracy, libraries, architecture, mathematics, astrology, biology, engineering, and more. Alexander would make these innovations known throughout the world.

Although many of his methods feel out of sync with our modern sensibilities and ethics, more than three hundred years before Christ, Alexander was on the cutting edge of leadership practice and culture craft. Through his leadership, we see demonstrated many timeless principles for creating an organization capable of changing the known world. He understood instinctively the power and opportunity of his role to engender trust and followership, as well as to build an enduring culture.

Among his greatest insights was the fact that his army always watched its leader. His understanding of this guided many of his actions we still talk about today. Among them is how, when his men had their horses shot out from under them and had to walk, Alexander dismounted and walked with them. When his men were without water, he would not drink; even when he was given the last of their rations, he poured it on the ground. But most famous is Alexander's insistence on leading from the front. He led the charge and was in the thick of fighting for all of his major battles.

In 334 BC, when Alexander was twenty-two years old, he began his eight-year campaign to conquer the world. His army consisted of thirty thousand foot soldiers and five thousand cavalrymen. He began in the Macedonian capital of Pella, and by the time he was done, the empire reached from Greece to India and North Africa. Along the way, he named more than seventy conquered cities after himself.[1]

Because Alexander always led the charge, he was in constant danger. But he knew his presence would inspire his men and that his courage would fuel theirs. His actions would give credence to the values he espoused, thereby Amplifying his Aspiration.

Living the Values

The Greek historian Lucius Flavius Arrianus describes one of the more harrowing examples—from 326 BC, eight years into the campaign—of Alexander's passion for leading from the front. The battle was set against the Mallians, people who occupied the region of modern-day Pakistan.

After capturing the fortified city, Alexander wanted to secure the acropolis as well. Feeling his men were moving too slowly to position the ladders, he took one himself and was the first to move toward the top, protecting himself from the onslaught of the archers with his shield as he climbed. Once he was atop the wall, without waiting for his men to join him, and still under attack from the archers, he leaped down into the citadel.[2]

Upon descending into the midst of the enemy, he kept many men at bay with his sword and found a tree to cover his back. During this phase of the battle, Alexander was struck by an arrow that entered just behind his breastplate and pierced his lung; it was a near-mortal wound. By all accounts, he was bleeding profusely and breathing from the gaping hole.[3]

"But although he was faint with exhaustion, he defended

himself, as long as his blood was still warm. But the blood streaming out copiously and without ceasing at every expiration of breath, he was seized with a dizziness and swooning, and bending over fell upon his shield."[4]

By this time, additional ladders had been secured, and his men came and rescued their wounded leader, the arrow still protruding from his side. Upon regaining consciousness, with no surgeon in their party, Alexander ordered his men to perform the surgery. He first instructed them to break off the shaft and then told his bodyguard to make an incision with his sword so the arrowhead could be removed. At this point, Alexander lost consciousness again. Fortunately, the arrow had not penetrated the thoracic cavity—if it had, he would not have survived. With the arrow removed, the process of recovery could begin.

Not only did Alexander survive to fight many more battles; in every assault, he could always be found leading from the front.

I am not sure what lessons you might take from Alexander's story. For me, the first time I heard of his courage, it made me stop and think. How might the world be different today if Alexander had merely *talked* about courage, bravery, and sacrifice?

More Caught Than Taught

I was told years ago: more of leadership is caught than taught; I believe the same can be said for values. Alexander's story appears to illustrate this concept well. His men saw courage, bravery, and sacrifice in the flesh. These were not abstract concepts or lofty ideals. Instead, their leader embodied these attributes. None of this means I am against teaching leadership—I have devoted my life to encouraging and equipping leaders through teaching. But the truth is, people need to *see* leadership much more than they need to study it.

This is why we have included this chapter, "Follow the Leader," as a primary strategy to Amplify the cultural Aspiration you have established for your organization. Would Alexander's men have fought to the death without his example? Perhaps. But would they have fought as gallantly? Would they have won? Some historians believe his example rallied his men to new heights. They were not just fighting for an idea or a concept, nor to follow orders. Their leader was with them, showing them what valor and courage looked like. They were fighting for *him*.

When we hear a story like Alexander's, we can easily fall into the trap of the grand gesture. The stakes obviously cannot be much higher than those of hand-to-hand combat. But it's important also to recognize the power of the mundane moments, the seemingly trivial actions, and the ordinary encounters. These mark our leadership. These moments happen all day, every day. Without thoughtful actions on our part, these opportunities will be wasted, missed, or worse. If we respond in a fashion contrary to our Aspiration, we can unwittingly undermine our efforts to create the culture we've been dreaming of. People always watch the leader. What are your people learning from watching you?

More Than Profits

I'll ask the question again: What are people in your organization learning from watching you? Perhaps they are learning the value of a good work ethic or professionalism or grit. All of this is fantastic, but they could learn so much more. They could learn generosity, service before self, or even compassion.

Marc Benioff founded Salesforce in 1999. The company has

been recognized as the Most Innovative Company by Forbes, as well as a Best Company to Work For and the tenth World's Most Admired Company by *Fortune*. Benioff's personal purpose is to contribute to the world around him. When he founded Salesforce, he thought this would be another vehicle for him to live out that purpose.[5]

Benioff is an outspoken activist, philanthropist, and author. He constantly demonstrates to his employees his commitment to execute on his vision of "improving the state of the world."[6]

In an organization of over 200,000 people, it would be hard to find an employee who cannot recall the vision of Salesforce. Benioff is known to spend over half of his time working on causes outside of Salesforce and expects his employees to give back as well. He has donated hundreds of millions to different causes—including a $100 million donation to the University of California San Francisco, to build its children's hospital.[7]

Salesforce's world-changing activities are not confined to its founder. As explained to employees, the organization practices a 1-1-1 model. Salesforce donates 1 percent of revenue, 1 percent of its product, and 1 percent of its employees' time to the community.

The impact of Benioff's living example of the Aspiration shows. To date, Salesforce employees have donated over 3.5 million hours of service to their local communities.[8] Thousands of other companies have also adopted the 1-1-1 model.

YOUR WORLD

Let's invest the balance of this chapter by thinking about your world. How can you leverage the irrefutable fact that people always watch the leader?

Remember: creating the culture you want in your organization is a multifaceted process. There are three rules. You need as much clarity as you can muster regarding your desired future state before you can strategically work to Amplify your Aspiration. What you are trying to build or create needs to be your cornerstone. If you don't have clarity there, anything you do will likely breed confusion.

Here are a few questions to guide your thinking about how to Amplify your Aspiration:

- What exactly are you trying to accomplish regarding your culture (purpose, vision, mission, ethos, values, etc.)?
- What specific action(s) can you personally take to Amplify these Aspirations?
- What are you currently doing that may be undermining your Aspiration?
- Who can help you assess how well you are Amplifying your Aspiration? If you really want to know how well you're doing, you can ask people: "What am I doing to make you believe that our purpose, vision, or mission is real and important? What am I doing to make you think our Aspiration may not be important?"

What Are Your Plans?

Where do you begin? As strange as this may sound, I recommend a look back as a good place to start your journey. Our past often holds insights and learnings that we can see in retrospect but failed to grasp in the whirlwind of the moment. It's time for you to conduct an opportunity audit.

The word "audit" may or may not create warm and fuzzy

feelings in you, depending on your past experience with auditors. Here is my take: an audit is an attempt to discern the truth about the past. As I wrote in my book *Smart Leadership*, the best leaders choose to Confront Reality. This choice allows them to stay grounded in the truth and lead from a position of strength. Give it a try.

Step One: Clarify the Aspiration. Jot down your Aspiration in whatever form works best for you—even a rough draft. This will give you something to evaluate your activities against. This is what you are striving to Amplify.

Step Two: Identify past opportunities. Look back over your calendar for the last thirty days. Identify specific activities you personally engaged in that *could have been* easily linked back to some facet of your Aspiration.

Step Three: Review your actions. Look at the list you identified in Step Two and ask yourself a simple question: How did I use this opportunity to Amplify our Aspiration?

Here's an example from my world. At one point, our organization had a core value titled "Customers First." We also had a practice for officers in our company to periodically take live customer calls. I remember one day when I was scheduled to take these calls. I was extremely busy that day, and for a moment I began to rationalize why it would be okay for me to ask a member of my staff to cover for me. Then I caught myself. Remember, people always watch the leader. What would people think and say if I talked about "Customers First" but failed to honor my commitment to the customer? Thankfully, I didn't allow my busyness to overtake my beliefs. At least in that moment, my actions Amplified our Aspiration.

Identify as many of these instances—when your actions were totally aligned with your Aspirations—over the last month as you can. You may also want to take a few notes on missed opportunities.

As we sharpen our critique of the past, we should be better able to see opportunities in our future. That's why an occasional audit can be helpful. That being said, you don't want to live in the past. To do so would be like trying to drive while looking out the back window of your car the whole time. A far more productive territory for you to explore will be to think carefully and strategically about your future plans.

Step Four: Seize Future Opportunities. Look at your calendar for the *next* thirty days. Identify as many opportunities as possible to Amplify some facet of your Aspiration.

While we were conducting interviews for this book, one CEO confessed to us his need to be more strategic in proactively and intentionally Amplifying his organization's Aspiration.

Under his leadership, the organization had become laser-focused on its values. However, during our conversation, he realized he needed to revamp the talk he was going to give later in the afternoon to new employees. His current draft did not include the values. Our exchange underscored the need for intentionality if we are to fully Amplify our Aspiration.

What are you doing in the next month that provides a ready opportunity for you to Amplify your Aspiration? Make a list, write it down, put the activities on your calendar, and then follow through with them to Amplify your Aspiration!

To jump-start your thinking, here is a short list of moments in which you can Amplify your Aspiration:

- Mentoring an employee
- Talking to customers
- Talking to suppliers
- Designing a training experience
- Meeting one-on-one with a team member
- Meeting with a team
- Conducting a performance review
- Speaking for an outside group
- Talking about the future
- Holding recognition events
- Coaching a team member

Here's a final thought on the topic of seizing opportunities. I was challenged by a leader of a global organization to share some portion of its vision (Aspiration) during *every* meeting. If specific topics directly related to the vision weren't already on the agenda or didn't come up organically, he encouraged me to close the meeting by linking what we had just talked about to the vision. If you cannot connect the content of the meeting to the Aspiration, why were you talking about the issue in the first place?

TALKING TRASH

At the end of a chapter featuring Alexander the Great and Marc Benioff, there is a chance I've miscommunicated something. Yes, there may be grand gestures in our lives that define our leadership forever, like jumping off a wall into the enemy and fighting hand to hand with the enemy. But this is not typically how the battle will be won or a culture formed. The victory will almost assuredly come in the mundane moments of your life and leadership.

As a leader, if you want something to be done, you have options. Many times, the right option is to ask someone else to do whatever needs to be done. However, there is another way that in some circumstances will be more effective in the long term and certainly more enduring. As I hope this chapter has demonstrated, sometimes the best answer is to show, not tell. People always watch the leader.

My organization is in the restaurant business. One of the things our guests value is cleanliness. There are systems, tools, and checklists to help our team members maintain clean and inviting environments. This is all good and necessary. But how do you Amplify the Aspiration for clean restaurants?

Our former CEO provided a vivid illustration and response to this question by picking up trash. This was powerful in and of itself, but to further Amplify the Aspiration, he did not just pick up trash on *our* property. I was with him when he picked up trash in a Walmart parking lot, at one of our competitors' restaurants, and many, many other times over the years. He made a habit of showing us what was valued.

This may or may not sound revolutionary to you, but believe me: people always watch the leader! If the leader picks up trash, others will as well. I visited another organization and observed one of its senior leaders stepping over trash on her property. I guess she was waiting on the cleaning crew to do its job. Behaviors like this can have a subtle and lasting effect, either good or bad.

One day, I was driving through my neighborhood when I suddenly stopped the car and asked my son in the passenger seat to open his door. He did so with a quizzical look, as if to say, "Dad, have you lost your mind?" I asked him to grab a piece of trash on the street so we could dispose of it properly back at our house.

Why do I pick up trash? Why did I encourage my son to pick up trash? Because a leader I respect picks up trash. There is something powerful about a leader who Amplifies the Aspiration. You can be that leader for your organization.

YOUR MOVE...

What are those closest to you learning from your example?

TELL ME A STORY

The most powerful person in the world is the storyteller.
—Steve Jobs

Within days of beginning this work on culture, our team was confronted with two differing worldviews: the anthropological and the organizational perspectives.

The anthropologist's perspective is more of a spectator's view. They believe you can observe culture, describe it, and on a good day begin to understand the complex interdependencies contained within it, but you don't create it.

By contrast, the organizational perspective is very different. It holds that culture can be created, re-created, and shaped as desired. We'll not go into these opposing views here—rest assured, we have done a deep dive in both domains in order to form the conclusions represented in this book.

The reason I mention these two ideologies here is not to point out their differences, but rather to highlight one of their most striking and compelling areas of agreement: in both worldviews, stories are at the heart of culture.

THE AGELESS STORY

Human beings have been telling stories for millennia. The first recorded stories can be found within the Chauvet Cave paintings in France, generally agreed to be about thirty thousand years old. The scenes, discovered in December 1994, were formed by pigments applied by hand, depicting an account of prehistoric life. The images include hundreds of animals representing thirteen different species, including mammoths, hyenas, bears, leopards, and rhinos.[1] I can imagine the stories these primitive drawings brought to life. Who knows? Maybe the story was an epic tale of man against nature.

What these people were attempting to do thousands of years ago, we are still doing today—trying to convey thoughts, feelings, and emotions, as well as trying to connect with and persuade others.

Today, the tools have changed perhaps more than we can even comprehend, shifting from cave paintings to social media. And storytelling has become democratized and globalized. We now have a platform for virtually anyone in the world to tell their story whenever, however, and with whatever frequency they desire. As of July 2021, 4.48 billion people are active users of social media.[2]

WHY STORIES MATTER

Why has storytelling survived throughout the ages? Why do we insist on preserving and enhancing this ancient, prehistoric mechanism for communication? Here are a few reasons why stories are so enduring:

Appeal to everyone. Stories are the universal language. They appeal to the young and old, educated and not, women and men, across ethnic and socioeconomic boundaries and across learning styles and preferences.

Enhance Memory. Organizational consultant Peg Neuhauser found learning stemming from a well-told story is remembered more accurately and for far longer than learning derived from facts and figures. And cognitive psychologist Jerome Bruner's research suggests that facts are twenty times more likely to be remembered if they're part of a story.[3]

Trigger our emotions. When we hear a good story, our body releases oxytocin, the same hormone our body produces when we experience trust and kindness.[4]

Engage our minds. Stories have an almost magical ability to engage our imagination. We find them to be irresistible. Good stories well told create their own gravity. Literary scholar Jonathan Gottschall comments, "Human minds yield helplessly to the suction of story."[5]

Create meaning. In his work on *public narrative*, Harvard professor Marshall Ganz describes how stories are particularly suited for creating meaning in ways that connect with human emotions and move people to action.[6]

Foster brain health. Millennia have passed since the Chauvet Cave paintings were created, yet evidence continues to emerge regarding previously unknown powers of story. There are now findings that storytelling in a group setting combats dementia, Alzheimer's, and depression. This application of storytelling is a part of reminiscence therapy, which, in addition to improving brain health, may also improve relationships.[7]

We are all part of a story, and most of us want to be part of a bigger story. This is where leaders come into the picture.

LEADERS AND STORY

In my book *Smart Leadership,* I wrote about many of the tools a leader has in their toolbox for creating change. I covered topics such as vision, accountability, structure, role clarity, planning, measurement, and probably a dozen others. Looking back, I talked a lot about communications—the need for messages to be thoughtful, strategic, and consistent. What I failed to point out is the power of story within a strategic communications plan.

I have talked for many years about the need for leaders to paint a compelling picture of the future. I have advocated for multiple intelligence theory as a concept every leader should embrace and master. What I have not done enough, however, is exalt the power of story to move the human spirit.

Steve Jobs maintained the worldview that "the most powerful person in the world is the storyteller." I'm not sure I am ready to agree completely with him, but a story well told can certainly change the world. The best leaders understand this power intuitively, which is why story is a tool of choice for leaders who want to Amplify their cultural Aspiration.

The Villain and the Hero

Jobs was one of the greatest storytellers in the world of business. His prowess was never more brilliant than when introducing a new product.

On January 24, 1984, Jobs was about to introduce the Macintosh at the annual shareholders meeting. But first, he wanted to establish some tension by introducing the villain. Here is how he began his presentation:

It is 1958. IBM passes up the chance to buy a young fledgling company that has invented a new technology called xerography. Two years later, Xerox is born, and IBM has been kicking themselves ever since. It is ten years later—the late sixties. Digital Equipment Corporation and others invent the minicomputer. IBM dismisses the minicomputer as too small to do serious computing and therefore unimportant to their business . . . It is now ten years later. The late seventies. In 1977, Apple, a young, fledgling company on the West Coast, invents the Apple II, the first personal computer as we know it today. IBM dismisses the personal computer as too small to do serious computing and therefore unimportant to their business . . . It is now 1984 [Jobs slows his pace and adds a bit of drama to his tone]. It appears IBM wants it all. Apple is perceived to be the only hope to offer IBM a run for its money. Dealers, initially welcoming IBM with open arms, now fear an IBM-dominated and controlled future. They are increasingly turning back to Apple as the only force that can ensure their future freedom. IBM wants it all and is aiming its guns on its last obstacle to industry control: Apple. Will Big Blue dominate the entire computer industry? [The audience shouts, "No!"] The entire information age? ["No!"] Was George Orwell right? ["No!"][8]

This story compelled the audience to action. Jobs cast the fight in terms of good and evil, an irresistible dynamic. No doubt, the roles were clear: "Of course we're the good guys! We must defend the world from the aggressor!" What else could they do?

Here's how author Carmine Gallo summarizes Jobs's talk:

> In the Steve Jobs narrative, the villain is a force that is aiming its guns at its last obstacle—the hero who is the last entity that can protect freedom. Is this a product launch or a script for a Star Wars–like movie? It's both, and that's why a Steve Jobs presentation was a mesmerizing experience. Jobs intuitively understood what great screenwriters know, and what great works of literature are made of: heroes and villains are the fundamental building blocks of a compelling narrative.[9]

A BETTER STORY

I've been on a personal journey to tell better stories for many years. One of these days, I may write a book on this subject. For now, I'll share a few tips I've come across on my quest.

Never tell a story. As I just referenced, I've been working on becoming a better storyteller for a long time. One strategy I've employed is to work with a coach—I've had several amazing coaches over the years, masters of the art of public speaking and storytelling. I've received coaching on pace, tone, content, openings, endings, props, gestures, and more. As I reflect on all of this feedback—received over many, many years—I think the most helpful, challenging, and thought-provoking advice I ever received was from Victoria Labalme, who challenged me to "never tell a story again."[10]

I am guessing this admonition hits you like it hit me . . .

bizarre! In any case, here I am years later, writing a chapter on storytelling—so what happened? Labalme's advice was confusing until I heard and understood what she said next: "Don't tell a story; *take* them there." I will admit the implications have taken a while to sink in.

Here's what Victoria told me. "It's as if someone early in your career told you, 'You need to tell stories,' so you do. However, it feels like you tell them so you can check it off your to-do list. You rush through them as if they are some obligatory gesture required of every speaker in every talk." What she did not know is that I had been taught as a young communicator to have "a point for the head and a story for the heart." Therefore, if I had three points, I assumed I needed three stories. This seemed like a good concept to me. Unfortunately for my audiences, the value of some solid advice was lost in translation.

As I began to explore what would be required to "take my audience there," several things began to change: my pace, my tone, my language, the level of detail. Regarding level of detail, I remember a session with Victoria in which I said, "A man came to the door." As I moved on, she said, "Stop, stop!" I was startled by her tone and her interruption. Confused, I did stop—to see if she was having a heart attack and if, perhaps, I needed to call 911.

In an animated tone and at a rapid pace, she began to rattle off questions. "Was he tall? Was he short? Was he old? Was he wearing a sweater? Was it a cardigan? Was it tattered? Was he wearing glasses? Was he Asian or Caucasian?" I replied, "Who?" Her response: "The man! You have not *taken* me there!" She made her point.

My advice to you is simply to do what Victoria suggested and "take your audience there." And don't use stories because you are supposed to; they are not obligatory. Use them thoughtfully and strategically, like how Rembrandt used a brush—with purpose and intent and attention to detail. If you do, everyone will see in vivid detail the man who comes to the door.

Tension is essential. Building tension is a storytelling technique as old as time. However, this was yet another facet of storytelling I learned rather late in life. I continue to relearn this every time I do a talk or write a blog post. Story only advances in the face of tension.

The first draft of one of my early books was a disaster. Don't get me wrong—all of my first drafts are bad—but this one was ridiculously bad. I shared the manuscript with a colleague, who I later learned had a master's degree in English. When she returned the "book," she said, "This is awful." I love the truth-tellers in my life. Having an extremely thick skin and being eager to learn, I asked her to please tell me more.

She proceeded to decimate the draft. She mentioned, among other things, "This is not even a story," which was particularly problematic because the book was a business fable. I was really confused. I replied, "Well, there are characters, and dialogue, and content . . . and 25,000 words." That's all I had to go on. She informed me that none of those attributes constituted a story.

I was still confused. She continued, ". . . and there is no conflict or tension. Without it, you cannot have a story, at least not a good one. The hero must encounter obstacles and barriers. The best stories have both internal and external conflict." I was taking notes as fast as I could. She asked, "Didn't you learn any of this in school?" Unfortunately, I had not.

After she was convinced my confusion was genuine, her tone

changed. Rather than being offended by my poor writing, she became determined to help me learn some of the basics every writer (and leader) should know—the elements of story!

Although a full exploration of this topic is beyond the scope of what we are trying to do here, I encourage you to become a student of story. For this section, I want to draw your attention to the need for tension. What problem are you trying to solve? What obstacle are you trying to overcome? Who is the villain in your story? In the Steve Jobs example above, he introduced IBM as the bad guy *before* he introduced the hero: the Macintosh. Be sure to have tension in some form or another, and you will tell better stories.

There must be a hero. Every great story has a hero. Now, you may be thinking that *you* are the hero. Be careful. Nancy Duarte, who leads perhaps the best visual storytelling business in the world, teaches communicators to be sure to make the audience the hero. You may decide that the hero is someone other than the audience—no problem, so long as you have a hero. Just make sure your audience has someone to root for and hopefully empathize with—someone who encounters and overcomes obstacles. If it does, your story has a much better chance of resonating.

Always be prepared. One day, a leader said to me, "I notice that you seem to always have a story, illustration, or anecdote to support your message. How do you do that?" First, I think he was grossly overstating my readiness. However, I did have a response for him: "I prepare." I encouraged him to invest time into thinking about the projects he was involved in, the principles and values he held dear, and the problems he saw on the horizon, and to proactively find the right stories, illustrations, facts, and examples to help him better communicate when opportunities presented themselves. Think of this like putting arrows in your quiver. You won't know when you will need them, but when you do, they'll be ready.

Never stop learning. If you are a leader, I encourage you to make storytelling a part of your ongoing, lifelong development plan. What does this look like? You get to decide! Here are a few tips to continue growing as a storyteller.

- *Look for stories everywhere.* When you find one, write it down. Pay special attention to stories from your own life and leadership.
- *Read books on storytelling.* At least one per year is probably a reasonable goal.
- *Find someone to help you.* Consider hiring a communications or public speaking coach. If your budget is limited, you can enlist a mentor to help you in this area.
- *Watch videos of yourself presenting.* Make notes on how you could improve your storytelling. If you find it too difficult to shoot videos or don't already have some recorded, audio will suffice—but you'll miss the nonverbal elements of your storytelling.
- *Interview people who are good at storytelling.* Prepare a dozen questions before your meeting to guide the conversation.

Many leaders tell stories every day. If you don't, you're leaving one of the most powerful tools at your disposal in the bag. If storytelling *is* a conscious part of your leadership, are you telling your stories well? How many of your stories are Amplifying your Aspiration?

Every leader can improve in this area. What might happen if you devoted yourself to becoming a master storyteller? My guess is your culture would be stronger, your influence would be greater, and you would be a better leader.

YOUR MOVE...

Which of the leaders that you know is the best at storytelling? Schedule a meeting with them and ask one question: What have you done over the years to improve your storytelling skills?

CREATE TOMORROW TODAY

You will never change your life until
you change something you do daily.
—John C. Maxwell

In addition to modeling your Aspiration and storytelling, there are other proximal levers you can use to help your message break through the clutter of a frenetic world. How you invest in others, how you interact with them, and what you choose to do on a day-to-day basis shapes people's view of your culture and your leadership. You are creating tomorrow today.

ONBOARDING

Many years ago, I heard Horst Schulze, former president and COO of the Ritz-Carlton, say something that challenged my thinking about how new people enter an organization: "The first forty hours on the job are the most important in an employee's career."

During the first week, the new person is exposed both to

what is professed and to what is actually practiced. They learn the real norms, expectations, and values. These new employees will also begin to assess their value in the eyes of the organization and evaluate the value proposition they were sold in the interview process—was it based on fact or fiction? They will also start forming their beliefs about the leadership.

Schulze knew all of this, and as a result, he personally conducted the initial onboarding at all the company's new hotels. Each time, he invested several hours introducing new employees to the culture and the expectations. He told them they were ladies and gentlemen serving ladies and gentlemen. Before the morning break, he would invite anyone who didn't want to be part of what he had been describing not to return after the break. Half-hearted, compulsory compliance would not be sufficient. He challenged them to go all in or go home.

Another organization fully committed to extensive and thoughtful onboarding is Disney. I have attended a portion of its multiday course, Disney Traditions, which provides an in-depth look at the company's history, purpose, values, and future. Full of storytelling and imagination, this course is required for all new hires, including both entry-level employees and senior leaders. For many years, the course was even required for contractors doing repairs on the property.

Jeff James, former vice president and general manager of Disney Institute, notes, "It's important for onboarding to go beyond just the '*how-to*' alone to also include an overview on *why* the organization exists and does what it does. By sharing the organization's common purpose and shared values, new hires can see how they fit into the company's culture and be reaffirmed in their decision to work for the organization."[1]

Onboarding and orientation are not the same. Orientation is typically an administrative process—new hires complete the necessary paperwork, sign several documents they probably didn't read, and pick up their name badges. This can be part of their onboarding but should not be considered complete. By contrast, onboarding done well is a cultural experience. It is the beginning of a never-ending inculcation process. This is when you begin to implant the DNA of your organization in the hearts and minds of new hires.

How strong and strategic is your onboarding process? Are you investing appropriate energy into the first forty hours for every new employee? At the end of their first week, what does the typical employee think about your organization and your leadership? Are they all in?

RECOGNITION

Every human being wants to be seen, known, and recognized by others. People want to feel as though their work matters and that they are making a difference. When you recognize people whose actions reinforce the Aspiration, you will reap more of the desired behaviors.

This is not a new concept. Over 2,300 years ago, Plato said, "What is honored in a country is cultivated there." The same is true in your organization. What elements of your cultural Aspiration are you honoring? How, and how often?

If you need any further convincing regarding the power of recognition, here are a few statistics.

- Eighty-two percent of US employees don't feel their supervisors recognize them enough.[2]

- Forty percent of US employees say they'd put more energy into their work if they were recognized more often.[3]
- Employee engagement, productivity, and performance are 14 percent higher in organizations with recognition than in organizations without.[4]

Let's close with another example from Disney. Although it does many things in the area of recognition, its Legacy Award is Disney's highest honor. This recognition is given annually to a select group of Disney employees from the ranks of cast members, crew members, and Imagineers. The candidates are nominated by their peers, and the recipients are celebrated for demonstrating three values.[5]

Dream: Going the extra mile every day to make dreams become reality and improve the Disney experience

Create: Developing new and effective initiatives to improve the workplace environment and upholding Disney brand quality

Inspire: Inspiring others with a positive attitude, constant support, and team spirit

Winners of the Legacy Award receive special blue nametags to proudly wear every day as they go to work.

What recognitions do you have in place to routinely and systematically Amplify your cultural Aspirations?

SYMBOLS AND TRADITIONS

There has been deep study in the field of psychology to understand why symbols and traditions have such a profound impact on human psyche and behavior. All I'll say here is to look for every opportunity to use their power to Amplify your Aspiration.

- **Symbol:** Something that represents or stands for something else, especially a material object representing something abstract
- **Tradition:** The handing down of information, beliefs, and customs by word of mouth or by example from one generation to another without written instruction[6]

It's About the Coffee

I am a huge fan of Starbucks. My family and friends will tell you I drink way too many venti mochas. I tell them I can stop any time I want to—I just don't want to. Not only am I a Starbucks customer, I am also a student of its operations. Although I have not counted, I would guess I have visited hundreds of Starbucks locations in cities all around the world, from Singapore to Cusco to Cannes, and untold locations in between. However, the reason Starbucks comes to mind as I think about symbols and traditions dates back to a trip I made to its corporate headquarters more than a decade ago.

At the time, I was responsible for our corporate communications efforts, and members of my team and I were in Seattle to meet with the Starbucks head of communications and members of her team. Just as we were about to begin the meeting, a woman entered, pushing a cart.

Our host announced that we would begin our meeting with some coffee and a tasting. I remember saying, "Thanks for doing this for us—what a thoughtful gesture." In a polite, no-nonsense tone, she said, "We aren't doing this just for you. We begin all our meetings like this. We want to be sure our people never forget we are in the coffee business. This practice also gives us a chance to educate and grow our team's knowledge about the product and the business."

While I was still processing all of this, the woman manning the cart began to tell us about the featured coffee we would be sampling. She was like a coffee sommelier. She told us about where the coffee was grown, how long this particular roast would be featured in stores, and more. Then, for the tasting, she explained that Starbucks had also selected a particular pastry to feature and recommend across its stores because it believed the product would be great with the featured coffee. In all, this little session took about ten minutes.

I decided not to press our host on the idea of doing this before *every* meeting—that sounded unbelievable. But when the woman with the cart left our meeting, she went down the hall to another one. I saw her later in yet another conference room. It's about the coffee.

Howard's Rock

Obviously, something like the coffee cart is time-consuming and expensive. But not all rituals, symbols, and traditions are costly. Consider the pregame ritual of Clemson Tiger football players.

In the early 1960s, someone gave Frank Howard, the Tigers' coach, a rock they had picked up in Death Valley, California. "Death Valley" was the nickname given to Clemson Memorial Stadium in 1948 by Lonnie McMillian, whose Presbyterian College team was regularly defeated by the Tigers in their home stadium. Death Valley has been an apt moniker for decades due to the Tigers' prowess at home—as of 2020, they won 75 percent of their games in the stadium.[7]

Howard's rock, a large piece of quartzite, made its first appearance at a game on September 24, 1966. Virginia was beating Clemson by eighteen points, with seventeen minutes remaining. Miraculously, Clemson rallied and won. From that day forward, the rock was deemed to have mystical powers.

The tradition of rubbing the rock as the players entered the stadium began in 1967. Howard reportedly said to his players, "If you're going to give me 110 percent, you can rub that rock. If you're not, keep your filthy hands off of it."[8]

What symbols and traditions do you already have in your organization? How many of them are linked explicitly to your Aspiration? What new activities could you begin to Amplify your Aspiration? You may find, like the Clemson players did years ago, that these types of routines can have a profound impact on culture.

Strategic Termination

I will conclude this chapter with a topic you may not have considered as a tool in your toolbox while building a High Performance Culture: strategic termination.

Let me be clear on this—I want to encourage you to select with care, onboard thoughtfully, and train, educate, develop, and coach people to succeed. I was challenged by our founder many years ago when he told me, "No one has ever built a successful career on firing people. You build your career by helping people be successful." I agree! However, from time to time, the most important and strategic thing you can do is fire someone.

In 1981, Jack Welch was the newly minted CEO of General

Electric, replacing Reginald Jones. The organization had a history of growth and change. Welch would accelerate both.

Early in Welch's tenure as CEO, he fired one of the company's most successful marketing leaders (we'll refer to him as Joe). The board was understandably disturbed. So they did what many boards do when they have a concern—they called an emergency meeting and summoned the CEO. They decided to meet in Crotonville, the company's training and development center in upstate New York.[9] (I've been there; the campus is spectacular.)

The board had convened in the Pit, the classroom with raked seating rising above the floor where the instructor would typically stand. The amphitheater design and the context for this meeting must have made Welch feel like he was entering the Colosseum to defend himself.

When Welch's helicopter landed, he went directly to meet them. Upon arrival, he spoke first. By all accounts, he said something like, "I know why you've called me here. I know you want me to explain why I fired a high-performance leader like Joe. It is really very simple."

He went to the board and drew his now-famous two-by-two model with performance on one axis and values on the other. He continued, "For us to build the future we all want, we need leaders in this quadrant." Pointing to the top right, Welch explained, "These people must be both high performers and be willing and able to champion our values. Joe's problem: he could produce the numbers, but he was unwilling to embrace our values. He had to go."

As Welch turned to walk away, one of the board members asked, "What about people who embrace the values but can't deliver the numbers?" Welch's response: "That's why we have Crotonville."

I have seen this dynamic play out over and over again. After a leader has made the hard decision to let someone go because they could not, or would not, embrace the values of the organization, the leader has told me how wonderful it was for their team and culture.

You have to decide how important your Aspiration is—really. Are you willing to do the hard thing and tell someone they will have to work somewhere else?

YOUR MOVE...

What can you do *today*, up close and personally, to Amplify your Aspiration?

WIN WITH PEOPLE

Great vision without great people is irrelevant.
—Jim Collins

How important is selection when thinking about culture? Peter Drucker said, "The most important decision a leader makes is who does what." However, it appears that many leaders around the world do not agree with Dr. Drucker.

During our research, we identified twenty-four potential drivers of culture. The list included items such as shared language; clarity of values; demonstrated diversity, equity, and inclusion; transparency around decisions; and many more. We then asked 2,124 leaders from around the world to rank these attributes. Shockingly, "hiring alignment with values" didn't even make the top ten when rated by US leaders—it came in at number fourteen.

I cannot imagine building a High Performance Culture without a significant focus on the people. I'll go a step further: you cannot build an enduring, great organization without adequate attention to the people . . . because they *are* the organization.

How should leaders think about people in terms of culture?

For me, this exploration has to begin with the question of fit. The concept of fit is not new, but far too many leaders have a limited view of this critical concept. There are at least two dimensions worth deeper examination.

FIT FOR ROLE

In the early 1960s, coach Tom Landry and the Dallas Cowboys began working with A. Salam Qureishi, a talented mathematician and programmer. Together, they created the first software capable of evaluating the performance of college athletes. This system and the thick binder of reports the program produced, called the "book," revolutionized the way coaches approached player selection. Up until this point, the process had been based primarily on hunches and brand names.[1]

A few years later, Bill Belichick and his defensive coordinator, Nick Saban, were introduced to this system, and from then on, the football world would never be the same. Belichick has won seventeen division championships and six Super Bowls as the head coach of the New England Patriots, while Saban took a different path and invested his talent in the college game, winning seven national championships . . . so far.

You may or may not be a college football fan. If you are, you are probably not a fan of Saban and the Crimson Tide of Alabama. There are countless reasons why you might not cheer for Alabama, but you can learn from them—I certainly have.

As a casual fan, I realized several years ago that Alabama was winning a lot of games (and national championships). Recently, I began to understand *why* they were winning so many games.

While doing research for my book on execution, *Win Every*

Day, I began to see some of what was going on behind the curtain that enabled Alabama's consistently high levels of play week after week and year after year.

Clearly, there are many factors enabling an organization to do what the Tide has done, and chief among them is leadership. However, we will not do a deep dive on leadership here. What we will focus on is the priority the best leaders place on selection. Who is on your team matters!

Building on what Landry and others began developing over fifty years ago, Saban and his staff have created their own version of the "book." Here is an excerpt from Phil Savage's excellent book, *4th and Goal Every Day*.[2]

The Crimson Tide defines the characteristics needed for a position and rarely strays from the definition. A football player needs to be a certain height and weight with the requisite speed for each position and needs the intangibles of character, competitiveness, and toughness.

Regarding position specifics, here are some of the requirements for linemen:

The arm length should be thirty-three inches or longer because your lineman needs to be the first to get hand placement on the other guy and steer that blocker or defender. You can give a little for guards and center and allow thirty-one and thirty-two inches with arm length, but tackles have to be at least thirty-three inches to reach defensive ends in the run game and protect the edge in the pass protection.

This illustration was a revelation and a challenge for me as a leader. The level of detail around the specific skills and attributes needed to excel in the Alabama system is staggering. This single idea has made me think very differently about fit for role. If you have someone who is not well suited for their specific role, success is impossible. Imagine a 340-pound athlete trying to play wide receiver. Crazy, right? Well, I have seen the equivalent of this folly in the business and nonprofit world my entire life.

Every person needs to have the ability to play their position with excellence. This does not mean they will join your organization with all the polish and poise you would like, but it does mean they must have the raw talent. Raw talent can be loosely defined as the basic ingredients needed for success.

If you need someone to interact with the public, and you have a candidate who really doesn't like people, you'll be in trouble if you select them. Or, if you need someone with high attention to detail, and the person in question has low attention to detail—as represented by their incomplete application or showing up twenty minutes late for their interview—you shouldn't expect them to suddenly develop a higher level of attention after they are on your payroll. The raw talent represents the table stakes that *must* be present for ultimate success in the role. If you are not clear on what those attributes are, you are probably not ready to make a selection.

Assuming you are clear on what is essential for success, then you can shift your focus to building skills. This is where coaching comes in—taking people with the necessary talent and helping them become great. Alabama calls this "player development."

But wait, this is a book about culture. What does fit for role have to do with culture? Great question. My answer is:

everything! You cannot become the organization you want to become if the people you select cannot excel in their roles. Fit for role is the first priority; however, this is only part of the equation.

FIT FOR CULTURE

After you have determined a person has the raw talent and the potential to develop the skills you need, you can then turn your attention to fit for culture. In some organizations, fit for role is determined by human resources professionals before the candidates are referred to teams or departments for interviewing. In these scenarios, the team leader or hiring manager is not trying to decide if the person can play the position. They are trying to answer the second, equally important question: Is this person a cultural fit? Regardless of who is responsible for what, someone needs to do everything possible to be sure a candidate is a fit for both role *and* culture!

Let's revisit the Alabama football program. As we already established, the young men who are candidates to join this elite team all have the physical attributes to excel at their positions. But the most important attributes can't be measured with a stopwatch or measuring tape: cultural fit and character. The men who are invited to join the team are also believed to be a culture fit. They are willing to work hard and be team players.

Here's how Saban himself describes a critical moment in the recruiting process: "[I say,] 'I don't want you to commit to Alabama,' and they look at me like I'm crazy. I say, 'I want you to commit to all the things that we're gonna do here to help you be successful as a person, as a student and as a player.'"[3]

Why do so many elite college athletes want to play for Saban? Alabama has sent more players to the NFL in the first round than any other university has over the last twenty years. Alabama has also won more national championships than any other school has during the same period. Excellence and the promise of a bright future are powerful recruiting tools.

So, why don't more organizations select for fit and culture? Some try, yet those who do often fail. The root problem is most organizations are awful at determining fit for culture. I don't know if this is a reflection of insufficient focus, effort, intentionality, discipline, or something else. We'll explore some possible root causes in a moment. Here's what the data tells us:

> Forty-six percent of new hires fail within the first eighteen months of employment, and of those failures, a remarkable 89 percent are due to personality or attitude issues—only 11 percent are for lack of skill.[4]

In other words, 89 percent of those who fail are not a fit for culture!

How do you explain such a poor track record for something as important as selection? No simple answer will suffice. It seems many leaders appear to believe the myth that efforts to select for cultural fit are futile, so it isn't worth trying.

If you look closely at the following, you will find an underlying mindset and accompanying assumptions. See if any of these sound familiar.

"Just hire their hands." This mindset probably has deep-seated roots going back over a hundred years. Of course, no modern-day leader will say "Just hire their hands" out loud, but in reality, every leader who ignores fit for culture is harkening back to Frederick Taylor and "scientific management."

In Taylor's system, the role of the worker was to work. The supervisors were to do the talking, and the leaders were to do the thinking. This way of running organizations was a byproduct of the Industrial Revolution and the advent of the assembly line. The challenges were compounded by the high number of immigrant workers, which created huge language barriers between workers and their employers. This led to an approach in which work was broken down into small, repeatable steps—executable without thought—and could be timed and measured, hence "scientific management." The legacy of Taylorism still looms over organizations today like a century-old hangover.

The cost of this mindset and approach is incalculable. The untapped potential, the stolen engagement, and the stifled creativity could transform the world—if leaders would change their approach. Thankfully, some have.

"Cut your losses." Some leaders take a laissez-faire approach to their hiring practices because of the perceived ease with which they can fix problems by just firing those who are not a good cultural fit. For many of you, I know you cannot imagine a leader taking this approach. But recall from the data above that 89 percent of employees were terminated in their first eighteen months because they were not a culture fit.[5]

I have actually talked to a leader who told me his strategy was to "hire and fire fast." He asks his leaders every week, "Who did you fire this week?" The cost of this approach is significant in a couple of ways.

One, the cost of turnover is much higher than most leaders want to admit. I know it is difficult to think about averages here because every situation is unique, but Gallup conservatively estimates the cost to replace and onboard a new employee to be one-half to two times their annual salary. In a 2019 report, Gallup estimated that voluntary turnover was costing businesses in the United States a whopping $1 trillion annually. Add involuntary separation, and you can do your own estimate regarding the cost.[6]

Next, the cost on morale to work in a place where someone is terminated every week must be staggering. Odds are good this is not a workplace known for high engagement.

Finally, and closely related to the previous point, high turnover makes it increasingly difficult to create a culture in which creativity, collaboration, and innovation can thrive. More than likely, people will not be interested in taking the risk necessary to deliver these outcomes if their leader has a "cut your losses" mindset.

"Only select the perfect fits." At first blush, this may sound like a great option, but there are a few problems with this strategy.

In the ongoing war for talent, finding enough people who are a *perfect* cultural fit is increasingly difficult. Besides, what is a perfect cultural fit, anyway? More on this question in a moment. Here's a related issue: if everyone is a perfect cultural fit, what happens when your new CEO or your existing leadership decides that you need a cultural transformation—a process increasingly deployed in organizations large and small?

Another downside of the elusive "perfect fit" is the tendency for this to be translated in practical terms to "sameness." "We can't hire him; he's not like us." Or, "She won't fit in because she's different." If everyone is the same, you won't have diversity or its benefits.

Strong cultures are aligned, but remember that the goal of alignment is not sameness; the goal is synergy. A great sports team is aligned in purpose, strategy, tactics, and even practice disciplines, but the players are different. A pitcher, catcher, and center fielder are *very* different athletes.

Organizations with diverse leadership and workforces are more successful over time. I'll share just one study to underscore this point. In a 2019 analysis, McKinsey found companies in the top quartile for gender diversity on executive teams were 25 percent more likely to have above-average profitability than companies in the fourth quartile—up from 21 percent in 2017 and 15 percent in 2014.[7]

Because the quest for the perfect fit is daunting, you may find that the pace of finding perfection is too slow to meet the growing demands of your organization. Take a look at your open positions. How many of them have been vacant for more than six months? A year? Could the problem be the pursuit of the perfect candidate?

"Hire culture-adds." Fortunately, not every leader has thrown in the towel on the issue of selection. There is an alternative to the approaches we just reviewed. This final mindset also hinges on what you believe about selecting for cultural fit. The leaders who choose this strategy have decided to use selection strategically as a mechanism to strengthen their culture—one selection at a time.

These leaders have a more progressive view of fit for culture. They believe every culture can be enhanced and every new hire is an opportunity to strengthen their culture. However, they are very careful not to define "fit for culture" as "just like us." Instead, these leaders look for "culture-adds."

Culture-adds are people who bring new experiences and perspective to your organization, adding richness and depth to your culture. In many cases, their background enables them to see things you don't, gain insights you might have missed, and expand your pool of talent beyond your current self-imposed limits.

Use your imagination. Think of the energy you could harness if you pursued a diverse mix of disciplines, industries, political views, faith traditions, socioeconomic circumstances, and more. These people will enhance your culture if they are fit for role and embrace your cultural Aspiration.

This entire section may have struck you as a blinding flash of the obvious. Of course you need to select players and employees who are fit for role *and* fit for culture. It is common sense, but as the old saying goes, common sense is not all that common.

First Role, Then Culture

Some leaders argue that it's best to start the hiring process by answering the culture fit question. Well, you can—but two things will likely happen:

- Your pool of candidates will be huge, and most of them won't be able to do the job well. If you start with culture fit, you will find tens of thousands, or maybe hundreds of thousands, or maybe millions of people who would be a good fit for your culture. If you are looking for a computer programmer with the latest skills, a huge percentage of those culture fits will not be qualified to fill your role.

- If your bias is to address culture first, you could also easily fall into the trap of "We'll teach them what they need to know." This is a noble sentiment, but if you are a

140-pound defensive end, even Alabama can't teach you to play the role well.

Here's the point I don't want you to miss: fit for role and fit for culture are *both* essential. My suggestion to screen the candidates first for their ability to do the required job is born of pragmatism and stewardship.

What happens if a person needs additional skills? You teach and coach them. That's why all great organizations, including sports teams, invest in training, development, and coaching.

Will a person successfully acquire the new skills and excel in a role requiring a different skillset? It's hard to say, but their chances of success skyrocket if their basic qualifications for the role were established before they were selected.

SIMPLIFY SELECTION

This section is built on the premise that you agree that fit for role and fit for culture are both essential. If you do, you are probably interested in learning some tactics to help you better search for both. Here are a few to jump-start your thinking.

Define the Win

What are you looking for in potential employees, exactly? Most of the job descriptions I have seen over the years are works of pure fiction. In many cases, they list every possible positive attribute, trait, and skill you can imagine. I'm not sure I've ever met a candidate that could check all the boxes. Have you?

Now, if you know specific non-negotiables, fantastic; you might as well document those. As I confessed previously, learning that

Alabama specified the required arm length of linemen stretched my thinking. If this level of detail helps you win, more power to you.

But if you only had a few broad categories to describe the essential attributes of your new hire, what would they be? Are all the people involved in your selection process aligned on these essentials? If you choose to have a shorter list of attributes or criteria, what are your top three? Are they all of equal weight and value? If not, rank them.

Probe for Your Values

This chapter is set in the context of Amplification—specifically, of Amplifying your cultural Aspiration. Therefore, the most essential and obvious first step is to be clear on the type of culture you are trying to build or fortify. Only then can you fully use your hiring process as a means to Amplify your Aspiration.

Qualtrics is a company specializing in survey software. It began, like many other successful startups, in a garage. The father-and-son team founded the company in 2002. Within the first five years, they grew revenue to almost $100,000 per month. Qualtrics is now worth more than seven billion dollars.[8]

When Qualtrics executives gathered to address the question "What describes us?," the team started by thinking about the people who were the "most Qualtrics," and why. What emerged are the Qualtrics values, affectionately known as TACOS:[9]

- **T**ransparent
- **A**ll In
- **C**ustomer Obsessed
- **O**ne Team
- **S**crappy

Born from the characteristics of the strongest employees, the Qualtrics values are an explicit cornerstone of company culture. As the company has grown, its leaders understand the importance of values-based interviewing to ensure candidates are best suited to enhance the culture rather than dilute it.

One of the principles our human resources people have drilled into me over the years is that the best predictor of future performance is past performance. Qualtrics understands this as well, so rather than asking candidates to merely respond to its values, the interviewer has conversations about how each person has demonstrated the Qualtrics values in their previous experiences.

Investing the extra time to assess cultural factors as well as core skill competencies has helped Qualtrics build a culture that attracts candidates from companies like Microsoft, Deloitte, and Google, bringing vast experience, diversity, and knowledge to its team.

How can you incorporate your values into your selection process? What other aspects of your Aspiration could you explore in your interviews? What about aspects of your ethos, purpose, or mission?

DEPUTIZE EVERYONE

Who needs to be aligned on how to select people who are both fit for role and fit for culture? Everyone involved in the hiring process, both directly and indirectly.

You probably get the "directly" part. Anyone who will conduct an interview, whether one-on-one or in a group setting, needs to understand the importance of Amplifying the culture with every new hire. In practical terms, this means they have:

- A thorough understanding of the cultural Aspiration
- Clarity on what types of people could be culture-adds
- Full awareness of the risks of sameness
- An understanding of bias and how to mitigate it as much as possible
- Clarity on specific position requirements
- Skills in behavior-based interviewing
- Alignment on any cultural non-negotiables (e.g., every new hire must have high learning agility)

The indirect part of this involves others in your organization. Often, people on the outside of the formal process can be a wealth of information. I think you would agree virtually everyone is on their best behavior when they step off the elevator on the human resources floor or when they meet the hiring manager. The more productive question: How do they behave in real life?

Have you considered sending a car to pick up candidates from the airport? If you do, be sure one of your employees is the driver. They can be a rich source of unvarnished feedback on the candidate. Who else interacted with the candidate? You should probably check in with your receptionist; ask them how they were treated by the candidate. You may be surprised at what you will learn.

———

In its most simple terms, culture is about aligning people around your Aspiration. You are not attempting to align machines. Human beings bring the cultural Aspiration to life . . . or not.

Think about your past experiences with people—I am willing to bet almost everyone reading this has encountered a situation when an individual was not a good fit for an organization. In some cases, it was a fit-for-role issue. However, if the data is to be believed, the vast majority of the time, the issues that lead to termination are fit-for-culture issues. There is only one smart way to attack this problem: make better selections. Not only will your culture be stronger, but you will also save untold amounts of time, energy, and cash.

If you select the right person—a new hire who is a fit for both role and culture—you win before they ever take the field.

YOUR MOVE...

How clear are you on *exactly* what you are looking for in your next new hire? Write it down.

ALIGN BY DESIGN

If you genuinely care about the goal,
you'll focus on the system.
—James Clear

I f you want to Amplify your Aspiration, the ideas from the previous chapters will help. However, these are not enough. You must also pull up beyond your daily interactions with people. What are the systems, processes, and policies you currently have in place that are helping or hindering you as you strive to achieve your Aspiration? How is your current governance and structure contributing to your culture? What are the issues awaiting your decision that will have far-reaching implications for your culture? You can have a tremendous positive impact on the alignment of your organization if you design the structural levers and mechanisms with care.

Earlier, we introduced our working definitions of structural and proximal influences on culture. This chapter is dedicated to a few ideas from the structural domain. These are changes that are typically controlled from senior levels of an organization and tend to have broad application and sweeping implications, while proximal influences are typically more personal, often demonstrated in one-on-one encounters with leaders or other members of the team. Unless you are a senior leader in your organization, you will likely need a little help using structural levers to Amplify your Aspiration.

WORKPLACE STRATEGY

One of the hot topics over the last few years has been remote work and the impact it has on organizational culture. A common refrain goes something like this: "Can organizational cultures survive in a remote or hybrid work world?"

Workplace culture has largely been place-bound since before the Industrial Revolution. However, this has been changing for some time. Remote work has been gaining steam for several years, as knowledge workers (including me, you, and millions of other professionals) realized we could literally work from anywhere. Many large corporations moved past requiring workers to "come to the office" several years before COVID-19. The pandemic forced many other organizations to make that same call. Now the debate regarding where people work has not only intensified, but these unprecedented circumstances also created a test of sorts—does entirely remote work really work?

Almost three years have passed since the pandemic began, and the early results are in: for many professionals, the vast majority of work can be done quite well without going to a centralized location. However, this revelation does not answer many of the lingering questions about the future of work.

How widespread is the desire for remote work? What are the personal costs of this strategy? What is the right balance of in-person versus remote work? What happens to collaboration? Will innovation suffer? What are the implications for organizational culture?

The consulting and accounting firm EY decided to probe into some of these thorny questions surrounding the future of work. Its survey received 16,264 responses from sixteen countries across twenty-three industries. Millennials represented more than half of all respondents. Here's some of what they learned:

> Nine in ten employees want flexibility in where and when they work. Given the choice, more than half of employee respondents (54 percent) would choose flexibility in *when* they work. By comparison, 40 percent want flexibility in where they work. On average, employees would want to work between two and three days remotely per week after the pandemic.
>
> When pandemic restrictions ease in their countries, 22 percent would prefer to work full time in the office, with 33 percent of employee respondents saying they want a shorter work week altogether. More than half (67 percent) believe their productivity can be accurately measured irrespective of location.[1]

Work is what we do, not where we go. This is now a fact, not a theory. Many organizations are also reporting record sales, profits, and productivity without the requirement for people to report to the office on a daily basis.

However, I want to raise a different question, not about sales or productivity. What about sustainability? The jury is still out on this question. I have no answers to offer—just a note of caution.

Human beings, professionals included, are social creatures. As leaders, we need to create a workplace strategy such that people can thrive and not just survive. We must be very careful not to assume a twenty-four-month uptick in productivity is the same as a new, long-term, sustainable way to do work in the future.

I continue to hear stories of loneliness, isolation, addiction, fear, anxiety, fatigue, exhaustion, burnout, and more. Certainly, all of these things existed when folks physically went to an office, but the intensity and frequency of these conditions appear to have increased. The early data supports my concerns.

According to the American Psychological Association's 2021 Work and Well-being Survey, 79 percent of 1,501 US adult employees experienced work-related stress in the month before the survey. Nearly three in five workers said work-related stress caused them to have a lack of interest, motivation, and energy at work. A total of 36 percent reported cognitive weariness, 32 percent reported emotional exhaustion, and 44 percent reported physical fatigue—a 38 percent jump from 2019.[2]

Without the boundaries of a physical place, many professionals are working too much. The lines were already blurry before the pandemic with our technology-driven, always-on culture. Now, without the limits gently imposed by a physical space, many people are working far too many hours in a given week. I've worked more hours than ever before in this new world; how about you?

Here's the question I'll leave you with as you contemplate next steps regarding physical-presence requirements: Is the level of productivity we've been observing during the pandemic sustainable? I doubt it.

Let's not misread the results of this recent season as sufficient evidence to change our long-term view of how work should be done. A leader should always be concerned with more than productivity. Viewed in isolation, productivity can create a mirage—a distorted and short-sighted view of reality.

What is the right way to do work in this new world, then? How do we best equip and empower our people to do excellent, life-giving work in a sustainable fashion? Here are a few ideas for you to consider:

Let your Aspiration inform your strategy. Think deeply about your cultural Aspiration. Does it include a *place* where people serve, are known, interact, and support each other physically? Is it a *place* where collaboration is the soul of innovation? Is your dream to build a *place* that people will be drawn to? If so, this will likely require some physical "together" time. Or does the work you do require so much collaboration and creativity that being physically together in order to excel at your craft is not an option? Maybe none of these is true of the products and services you provide.

Perhaps your Aspiration is more about the outcomes—such as how much code someone can write in a week, or how many calls a person can make or respond to in a day—and, therefore, the methods are of less concern. If this is your situation, being together is perhaps less critical. Create a workplace strategy that helps fulfill your Aspiration.

Provide tools, resources, and training. If you want people to work remotely, be sure they have what they need to be successful. As the world has learned, working from home is a complicated assignment for some people. Do they have the space? In particular, do they have a distraction-free space? Are they attempting to share their new workspace with someone else? Do they have access to high-speed internet connections? Do they have the necessary equipment? Do they need a desk and a chair? Do they need a monitor? Do they have the software and tools to meet and collaborate remotely? Have you set appropriate boundaries? Separating home and work was already challenging for many people before the pandemic when they were commuting to work. Boundaries and clear expectations are now more important than ever. Remember, the goal is excellent work *sustained* over time.

Overcommunicate your intentions. After only two years of the new world of work, there are some things we've discovered: remote and flexible work can be exciting, potentially confusing, and also frustrating. All of these descriptions can be true at the same time! My advice to leaders who are trying to figure out the new rules of work is to overcommunicate. Even if you don't have all the answers—which you don't—communicate with your people regardless. Tell them what you think you have figured out and what you have not. Also, I would suggest every iteration be seen and communicated as an experiment. When the results are in, share them. Then tell people what you are going to try next. The journey to the future is not going to be a straight line.

Listen, listen, listen. Think about all the strategies in your business. Most of them have changed over time; this is one of the characteristics of strategy people tend to forget. They are created at a point in time to help your organization pursue a goal or objective. If the context changes, you decide to set a new goal; or if the strategy fails to produce the desired result, you modify it or create a new strategy all together. The same needs to be true regarding your workplace strategy. Hold it loosely. The way you will know if it needs to change is by listening to your people—both what they say out loud and what they say silently with their actions and their work.

Embrace flexibility. Different types of work require different types of spaces. Different projects require different resources, including space. Some work requires face-to-face, in-person interaction; some does not. For most of you, your employees are not the workers scientific management was built upon. You need them to do a lot more than just work and meet their daily quota of widgets. You need them to think, engage, and grow. Don't make your work harder than it has to be with arbitrary and outdated norms or expectations. Leaders must always maintain flexibility in their thinking and their approaches to workplace strategy.

STRATEGIC COMMUNICATION

Strategic communication is one of the most powerful weapons in your arsenal for building a High Performance Culture. Many of you already have a more-than-adequate communications infrastructure in your organization to Amplify your Aspiration . . . if you will use it to that end. What's missing, in many cases, is intentionality, frequency, and constancy. So, please consider this section a friendly reminder.

When I use the word "strategic" in this context, I am talking about thoughtful, planned, multichannel messaging, designed and repeated to reinforce the core messages to your target audiences as required to strengthen your culture.

Where to begin? You should start by thinking about your Aspiration. What are the elemental components you want to be true in your organization? How can you share and illuminate these ideas? Who are the various audiences and stakeholders who need these messages? What channels will work best to reach them? What is the ideal frequency? Who are the best messengers for each audience and message? What historical biases are you attempting to overcome? How do you deputize other messengers (e.g., all leaders)? How do you keep the message fresh? What will be required to make the message evergreen? What competing or conflicting messages must you address? How do you help people internalize and personalize the message? Who is accountable for answering all these questions and executing the plan? These are just the questions to start the process!

Every organization's communication plan will be unique—like a strand of DNA, each one will bear the marks of its owner. What works for one group will almost assuredly need to be altered if it is to work somewhere else.

Here is an example of a high-impact nonprofit organization that is putting its own spin on what a successful strategic communications effort looks like.

Untold is an organization led by my oldest son, Justin. It serves those infected with HIV/AIDS in East Africa. In far too many cases, these people have been marginalized by their family, friends, and society. Untold exists to embrace and equip people to live a life beyond AIDS. Untold's staff of almost three hundred indigenous people have graduated more than thirty thousand people from their nine-month program. Justin is my hero.

As I reflect on the impact of this organization on the world, I am tempted to cite Justin's mother's genes and his own hard work; both are undoubtedly contributing factors. But the Untold team quickly came to mind as an organization working hard to leverage strategic communications to build a High Performance Culture.

Here are some of the strategies and tactics the organization has utilized to date:

- Effective website messaging (untold.org)
- Blog posts highlighting its Aspiration and its progress
- Engagement on several social media platforms
- Weekly staff meetings (in the United States and Africa)
- Annual staff retreats in which purpose, mission, and values are featured and celebrated
- Handwritten notes for and frequent contact with individual donors
- Amazing print materials with information about the state of the organization
- Personalized letters of appreciation to donors from program participants
- Annual trips to the United States by Kenyan national directors to give firsthand reports from the field
- Events to connect with donors and potential donors (in both large and small group settings)
- Email newsletters to external stakeholders and staff
- Webinars and virtual events broadcasting from both the United States and Africa
- Compelling, professionally produced videos showcasing both the need for and the fruit of their efforts
- Videos shot on cell phones by staff in the field and sent to donors to present a more real-time report on their work
- Frequent trips for donors and potential donors to see the work in Africa in person (as of this writing, more than 750 of Untold's supporters have traveled to see its work firsthand)

- Annual and multiyear giving campaigns
- Publication of *Beyond Blood*, a book about Untold's origin story
- Publication of *100 Faces*, a book featuring clients' success stories

You may look at this list of activities and see a fundraising infrastructure. If so, you would be correct. In the case of Untold, the work is 100-percent donor funded. There is no other economic engine. Look more closely, and you will see how its collective communications effort has created a community of people who have embraced the values, purpose, and mission of the organization. Untold's culture now includes its clients, staff, *and* its donors, each receiving targeted messages designed for them. Untold is using strategic communications to Amplify its Aspiration and to make it a reality for people halfway around the world.

FINANCIAL INCENTIVES

Financial incentives are an interesting and sometimes controversial topic. Virtually every leader has an opinion based on their own experience and biases. Based on the research, there is both promise and peril lurking behind the simple idea of paying people for the behaviors you want. This appears to make perfect sense, but unfortunately it is more complicated than it looks.

Let's begin on a positive note: there is a growing body of data indicating financial incentives *can* have a positive impact on *group* behavior. The operative words in this statement are "can" and "group."

The work of organizations is now more complicated and

complex than at any other point in history. One of the many byproducts of this state of affairs is the necessity for the work within an organization to be increasingly collaborative and interdependent. Therefore, incenting the whole for key outcomes is proving to be a successful approach. Giving people a stake in the key outcome(s) of an enterprise can drive ownership behaviors, employee satisfaction, and overall performance.

Importantly, the metrics you reward must be aligned with the outcomes you really want and drive value for the organization. If you incent the wrong behaviors, you will get the wrong outcomes. Also, if the items you reward are perceived to be largely outside of people's control, you won't receive the benefits you desire from the financial incentives.

Sounds good; what could go wrong? Well . . . as it turns out, a lot.

Although financial incentives continue to be a tool of choice when attempting to drive a wide array of outcomes—from share price to diversity, equity, and inclusion targets, to profitability, to culture—the science behind incentives is sobering yet largely ignored in business circles. I am not suggesting incentives will not drive short-term behaviors; I am suggesting they are not the cure-all most leaders are searching for.

The most interesting part of the incentive paradox is how science has proven that, for tasks with complex steps and solutions, incentives both do *not* work and often *reduce* the desired output. If the job at hand requires creativity, exploration, lateral thinking, or other right-brain activity, financial incentives are a deterrent to performance.

The research on this first emerged in 1962 when Princeton University psychology professor Sam Glucksberg ran experiments using incentives to drive participants to solve the classic "Candle Problem," which requires creative and outside-the-box thinking to find a solution. Simply put, the results were resounding: incentives blunted the performance of the participants.[3]

In a study commissioned by the US Federal Reserve in 2005, research led by psychologist Dan Ariely from the Massachusetts Institute of Technology, along with colleagues from the University of Chicago and Carnegie Mellon University, reached a similar conclusion. They conducted a series of experiments of their own design in the United States and in underdeveloped parts of the world confirming Glucksberg's findings. Here is what they said.

> [A]s long as the task involved only mechanical skill, bonuses worked as would be expected: the higher the pay, the better the performance. But when we included a task that required even rudimentary cognitive skill, the offer of a higher bonus led to poorer performance.[4]

One more note: the London School of Economics conducted a meta-analysis of fifty-one pay-for-performance studies. Its findings mirrored the conclusions of Glucksberg and Ariely.

> We find that financial incentives can result in a negative impact on overall performance.[5]

What's going on here? What's the difference between creating ownership behaviors or performance gains and the suggestion that financial incentives have a negative impact on performance?

The concerns expressed by many of the experts above focus

on *individual* pay-for-performance schemes. If you want to use financial incentives to drive the right behaviors within your organization, think about the whole enterprise, not individuals—unless the individual tasks are simple and mechanical in nature. If that's the type of work your organization does, pay by the piece may be your answer.

My summary regarding financial incentives is simple: be careful. They can be used to Amplify your Aspiration or constantly war against it.

———

Proximal and structural influences impact every culture. You have opportunity and responsibility in *both* of these areas.

Don't miss the power of individual, personalized, one-on-one influence. You are a champion of the culture, and your actions speak volumes. People always watch the leader.

At the same time, you and your fellow leaders should always consider the cultural implications of the structural decisions you make. Sometimes you will not know the impact. In many cases, there will be unforeseen consequences of your decisions. That is one reason why the third rule of culture, covered in the next section, matters.

You must always be willing to Adapt. In some of these situations, you will be proactively Adapting to enhance the culture. Other times, you will be addressing the unintended consequences of previous structural decisions you initiated.

In either case, we leaders should be thankful to have so many levers at our disposal to Amplify our Aspiration. Use them wisely.

YOUR MOVE...

What are some of the more successful structural mechanisms your organization has used to Amplify your Aspiration? What do you currently have in place that may be working *against* your Aspiration?

Rule #3

ADAPT

Always work to enhance the culture.

CHAMPIONS CHANGE, TOO

Better people make better All Blacks.
—Brian Lochore

The players were devastated, the coaches were wrecked, and the nation was inconsolable. Their team had just finished last in the 2004 Tri Nations Series with an embarrassing defeat at the hands of South Africa, 40–26. What happened next was perhaps the literal bottom of the barrel for this hundred-year-old storied team.

Once back at the hotel, the team held a mock trial fueled by large quantities of alcohol. As a result, some players had to be rescued from the hallways, bushes, and gutters and be placed in the recovery position by players from other teams. This was the state of the team in 2004, but these were *not* the All Blacks the world had come to know and respect.

The New Zealand All Blacks are a professional rugby team founded in 1903. They played in their first international competition in 1905 and overpowered their first opponent, Devon, with a commanding 55–4 win. Was this a fluke? They won their second match 41–0 against Cornwall and won their next game, too. What was going on?[1]

This was a startup rugby team from a country with no pedigree in the sport. The rugby world was shocked when the "Originals," as the team back then was sometimes called, earned an international record of 35–1 at the end of their first season. Their one loss was against Wales on a controversial last-second call. What the world did *not* know was that this was just the beginning of a sporting dynasty that would span more than a century.

So, what was happening in 2004 with men literally passed out in the streets, experiencing defeat in a fashion never before endured by their predecessors? The short answer: the leadership—players, coaches, and ownership—had failed to Adapt the culture of the organization. They had failed to proactively respond to the dark side of prolonged success and its traveling companions: apathy and entitlement. They had failed to understand what so many leaders around the world also fail to grasp—that the successes of yesterday are no guarantee of tomorrow's. Your previous wins are more likely a liability to be managed than a birthright to be cherished. The culture of the All Blacks enabled their past success—but it had to change if they were to continue to be the world's dominant rugby team.

THE ALL BLACKS ETHOS

New Zealand is a small and relatively young country, but thanks to the All Blacks, it is known internationally for rugby. The fascination with the team is hard to comprehend. Children across the country dream of being part of the team.

What creates this passion? Among the team members, a deep-seated sense of legacy is never far from their hearts and minds. The players believe they are playing for their country, families, and ancestors. Specifically, their "why," according to the New Zealand Rugby Union, is to "Unite and inspire New Zealand."[2] Each player is also given the charge to "leave the jersey in a better place" than when they received it. These two ideas capture the essence of their Aspiration.

How does the team Amplify its Aspiration? There are far too many examples to cover here. However, I'll share some of my favorites.

Opposing teams are confronted with the team's deeply held sense of purpose before every match. The All Blacks line up to perform a haka called "Ka Mate," originally composed by Ngati Toa chieftain Te Rauparaha around 1820. The haka is a ceremonial group dance in Māori culture and is popularly associated with traditional battle preparations and war cries. If you haven't seen one, you can do a quick Google search—they are intense.

According to author James Kerr, opposing teams face the haka differently:

Some try to ignore it, others advance on it, most stand shoulder to shoulder to face it. Whatever their outward response, inwardly the opposition know that they are standing before more than a collection of fifteen individual players. They are facing a culture, an identity, an ethos, a belief system—and a collective passion and purpose beyond anything they have faced before. Often, by the time the haka reaches its crescendo, the opposition have already lost.[3]

One other long-standing hallmark of the All Blacks has been their focus on the fundamentals of the game. They are known to practice the basics more than any other professional club does. Their discipline to master even something as simple as catching and passing is legendary—in a famous 2013 match against Ireland, while in injury time, they passed dozens of times on a single play to score in the final seconds for the win.[4]

Another defining attribute of the club, which has risen to mythical proportions, is its physical toughness. Every rugby team talks a tough game, but the All Blacks elevate the expectation for toughness to an entirely different level. The story of one incident, referred to as the Battle of Nantes, is chilling even to this day.

Early in the match, a Frenchman's boot raked and ripped Buck Shelford's scrotum. According to one account, a testicle was showing. Shelford limped to the sidelines, and a medic sewed up the wound without anesthetics! Shelford then returned to the game. He later had to come out of the game, not due to the previous wound, but because he was concussed and missing teeth.

All Blacks are expected to sacrifice for the team. In a sense, this has been the case since 1903; the All Blacks' results would make you think so. However, the vocalization of this sentiment and the modern-day mantra comes from Brad Thorn, one of the most accomplished players in the history of the sport. He says his father taught him: "Champions do extra."[5]

This became a guiding philosophy for Thorn and his teammates. Extra reps in the weight room, extra minutes on a run, extra passes in a drill, and more. This has become a trademark discipline for the greatest rugby team, perhaps the greatest team in any sport, of all time.

With a culture of purpose, passion, heritage, commitment, and personal sacrifice, and an obsessive focus on execution, what could go wrong? Almost everything.

THE REBIRTH OF A CHAMPION

Let's return to the devastation, brokenness, and agony following the Tri Nations tournament. The question the team faced was straightforward: "What went wrong, and where do we go from here?"

When everyone's minds cleared after the "trial," they agreed this was no temporary slump. Even the concept of a slump was something the team had little experience with. With their new-found clarity that something, perhaps many things, needed to change, everyone stepped up. They realized the team was in bad shape. Its collective heart had stopped beating.

According to Kerr, "We shouldn't be too surprised that the All Blacks culture had begun to rot from the inside. Unless intervention occurs, all organizational cultures do."[6] I agree; all healthy cultures Adapt. Those that don't eventually wither or implode.

During this challenging period, the team began to do some soul-searching regarding what needed to change and what did not. Interestingly, during these dark days, the haka was on the ropes; the team had lost the passion and meaning associated with this century-old ritual. Some players believed it was just for the camera and the fans, not for the team. Although no one said it out loud, the sentiment was clear: "We don't need an ancient ritual to win games; we are the All Blacks." Sustained success without proper perspective often breeds arrogance and complacency.

This debate around the haka illustrates the depth of the problems the team was grappling with. Could they Adapt sufficiently to rescue their culture? What would be required of them? Was the team too far gone to be saved?

They decided to address the heart of the issue: Why did they exist as a team? Why did they play? Why did it matter?

After hours of debate and even more personal reflection, one of the All Blacks' early decisions in an attempt to return to world dominance would be to affirm their Aspiration—they would not change their purpose, but they could refresh how their Aspiration was expressed. They would Adapt.

The team took a very proactive view of what it means to Adapt, going so far as to write its own definition: "Adaptation is not a reaction, but a systematic series of actions. It isn't just reacting to what's happening in the moment, it is being the agent of change."[7] Everyone was very serious about saving their culture and their team.

The team brought in Māori artist Derek Lardelli to help the players write a new haka, one connecting them to *their* purpose. They call it "Kapa o Pango," and it was performed for the first time in 2005.[8]

Let me go back to my first gasp of breath
Let my life force return to the earth
It is New Zealand that thunders now
And it is my time!
It is my moment!
The passion ignites!
This defines us as the All Blacks
And it is my time!

It is my moment!
The anticipation explodes!
Feel the power
Our dominance rises
Our supremacy emerges
To be placed on high
Silver fern!
All Blacks!
Silver fern!
All Blacks!
Aue hi!

Even in this bold move to rewrite a two-hundred-year-old haka many still considered sacred, the All Blacks exercised judgment; the traditional haka would not be replaced. The team now has *two* hakas, and the players have discretion regarding which one will be performed at any given game.

They also decided they wanted to ramp up their intensity on player development. They adopted a philosophy of "Better people make better All Blacks." With this mantra, they increased their attention on the mental aspects of the game.

The decision was made to think differently and more strategically about continuous improvement. In the end, the team decided to focus on three levels: structural (e.g., season and World Cup cycle), team (e.g., player selection and practice regimen), and individual. At the individual level, each player created a profile made up of seven to eight pillars, which translated to a daily map of self-improvement labeled "Things I Do Today." These activities informed their training and development on and off the pitch. Remember, better people make better All Blacks.

What does the story of the All Blacks teach us? For me, many things. But chief among them: when leaders are willing to Adapt, not react, to a changing world, they can build or rebuild a High Performance Culture. Today, the All Blacks are back to their winning ways, having won 77 percent of their matches.[9]

What is the state of your culture? People may not be lying in the gutters after a devasting defeat, but signs of culture rot could still be present. What interventions are needed for you to maintain, enhance, or create for the first time your own High Performance Culture? How do you need to Adapt?

RULE #3: ADAPT

One of my favorite advertising campaigns of all time is from Nike. The ads featured the slogan "There is no finish line." This idea captures the way I see life. It also embodies the spirit of the best leaders when they think about the culture of their organizations.[10]

If you follow the first two rules successfully, you will be ahead of the pack . . . for a while. Perhaps you can have a hundred-year run of success, like the All Blacks. Unfortunately, with the pace of change in the world today, most organizations cannot rest culturally for a century without the need for change. The third rule of culture building sets you up for long-term success.

Adapt: Always work to enhance the culture.

Admittedly, this third rule to constantly Adapt is a tricky proposition. Let's go back through the first two rules and see why the third rule is so challenging.

You fixed your heart and mind on a challenging Aspiration. You Amplified the Aspiration, and much to your delight, you began to see it become a reality. People went from talking about something to doing and being something. If we allow our finite brains to reach the conclusion that we are done at this point, then we *are* done.

We can never stop enhancing the culture. Employees come and go, technology changes, the needs of the organization change, our customers change . . . the world changes! All of this and more creates the need for leaders to lead the charge. Our organizational culture must Adapt.

We must honor the third rule—we must diligently monitor and enhance the culture *forever*. Translated, this means we must always listen, learn, and change. I have seen leaders dig in their heels at this point. "Change?" they ask. "We just got the culture where we wanted it to be!" The danger in this mindset is real. General Eric Shinseki summed it up well: "If you don't like change, you're going to like irrelevance even less."

Here's another way to think about it. Few leaders would assume their product or service offerings could remain fixed for an indefinite period of time. Market forces, competitive pressures, changing customer needs and expectations, and more create the need for change. The assumption that hard goods and services must morph, change, and improve over time is universally accepted. The same should be true for your culture.

The world is a dynamic place. For our organizations to thrive, we must be open to ideas and practices that are different from those of the past. As I said, this is tricky. I love the way Jim Collins talks about this in his book *Built to Last*: "preserve the core" and "stimulate progress."

The question you and I must constantly be asking as leaders is this: How can I enhance our culture?

How do you know what needs to be enhanced? Or which practices need to be tweaked, reengineered, or abandoned? This third rule requires discernment and diligence, especially if things are currently going well in your culture. A casual, haphazard, sporadic attempt to discern the pulse of the organization will prove inadequate. You will learn more about specific moves you can make in this arena in the following chapters.

The journey ahead will not be without trials and setbacks. This is to be expected. Teams and organizations do not drift toward greatness; they must be led there.

YOUR MOVE...

Which part of the All Blacks' story could you relate to? What actions could you take to avoid the kind of crash they experienced?

SCALE YOUR LISTENING

Stop and listen. The story is everywhere.
—Thomas Lloyd Qualls

One of the lessons we can learn from the All Blacks is the inherent danger when a culture fails to Adapt. Think about how close the All Blacks came to slipping into the oblivion of mediocrity. Have you seen this happen before? Some leaders see culture like a jigsaw puzzle that you work tirelessly to assemble, and then once it's completed, you're done. You believe your job then becomes to protect the finished product.

I remember a long time ago my mom worked diligently to complete a large puzzle and couldn't stand the thought of putting it back in the box. Then, she had the idea to laminate it. Once the plastic was stretched tight, all the air sucked out, what she had been so proud of immediately lost its beauty—the colors, once vibrant, were now reduced to muted hues by their shiny plastic protector. If you try to laminate, shrink-wrap, or freeze-dry your culture, it will lose its wonder and vitality. The culture you love— the beauty you are attempting to protect—will invariably be lost.

Cultures are comprised of human beings in a dynamic world.

The old saying "Change is the only constant" is real. Leaders who attempt to violate this law of the universe find themselves on the losing end of this battle. In the culture-building game, leaders are playing in an ever-changing reality. If you move into protection mode, you may feel a sense of satisfaction for a season. Then, probably slowly, your organization will become increasingly irrelevant and unable to meet the demands of a changing world. This challenge is at the heart of the third rule: Adapt.

To Adapt is an ongoing, never-ending effort to enhance a culture. To many leaders, this part of the game presents the greatest challenge. If you are not vigilant in this phase, you run the very real risk of losing all your previous gains. Even if the concept of ongoing enhancement makes sense to you, you may be wondering how to actually do it. To Adapt well always begins with listening well.

BEASTS OF BALANCE

The challenge of how to Adapt wisely and strategically reminds me of a new game my grandkids received for Christmas: Beasts of Balance. If you have not played the game, let me give you a quick overview (with a few culture-building parallels).

The individual players (leaders) are attempting to build a tower (organization). There are many individual pieces, each with its own unique shape, size, and characteristics (like the people in your organization). The players (leaders) work together to decide how the pieces should be stacked (like the structure in your organization). These decisions are largely formed based on the shape and functionality of the pieces (maybe a good strategy, maybe not).

Here's the twist I didn't mention: all your moves are being monitored on a smartphone app. Its real-time dashboard records the consequences of every move you make—just as in our world as leaders, virtually everything we do in the realm of culture will also have a ripple effect. In the game, the way to maximize points, as measured on the app, is not the height of the tower but the strength of the structure.

Interestingly, in our organizations, we often lack clarity on the real goal; many times, it is not what we think it is. The goal of Beasts of Balance is to build something strong and enduring, just like the goal in our organizations is to maximize long-term health, sustainability, and performance—not just to build something big. "Big and tall" is not the same as "enduring and great." It's interesting to watch individual players lose sight of the goal; many have trouble escaping their assumption that the taller the tower, the better.

While all this building is going on, your phone not only keeps score but also alerts you to the consequences of your moves. The app notifies you if one of your previous moves endangered another part of the tower and gives you time to take appropriate countermeasures.

All of this is taking place while you try to build a tower stable enough to stand on its own—and, by the way, some of the moves are timed, so if you don't exhibit sufficient urgency, or if the tower falls, you lose (i.e., your organization goes out of business).

Beasts of Balance is a powerful metaphor for what you are trying to do in your organization. I don't think I could have fabricated a better one. So, why tell you all of this?

Let's go back to a key component of the game and the single

factor most directly linked to your success. In Beasts of Balance, the secret to maximizing your score is the information provided by its mobile app. This feedback helps you thoughtfully and strategically determine your next move. Your phone monitors the health of your tower (organization).

What can leaders do to set up their own culture-monitoring mechanisms to stay in touch with the status of their culture? How do you listen at scale? This is the subject of this chapter.

THE LOST ART OF LISTENING

What can you do to monitor the health and vitality of your culture? The answer is not a mystery nor a surprise: listen.

Why is listening hard? We all have two ears and one mouth; it should be natural to listen twice as much as we talk. But if it were this simple, Adapting our cultures would be much easier. Here are a few of the challenges to listening well from an organizational perspective.

Noise in the system. There is a lot going on in the modern corporation. Have you ever considered how many emails you receive in a given year? The data indicates the typical office worker receives over one hundred emails a day![1] And for many, the number of text messages per day outpaces emails. You can see in these two channels alone the blizzard of information bombarding our people. Add to this meetings, distractions, social media, and a multitude of other issues, and you can visualize the challenge opposing our good intentions to listen well. If we are not careful, important signals regarding the health of our culture can be lost in this raging storm.

Personal and organizational bias. What we see is never a function of actual data or pure reality. The inputs we receive are always filtered by our role, prejudice, experience, personality, and our biases, both known and unknown. This is one of the most significant problems we face, and it makes listening well a huge challenge. Our own research indicated leaders see the world differently than the typical frontline employee does. As mentioned earlier, when asked if they would recommend their organization as a great place to work, leaders said yes about 67 percent of the time; individual contributors said yes about 27 percent of the time. This gap is a product of bias and differing perceptions of reality.

Insufficient frequency. Even with the best intentions, most corporate listening efforts fail the frequency test. Imagine if you only looked at your bank records or listened to your spouse once a year. Many organizations do an annual survey to check on their culture. Some do these listening "events" every two years, and some never use a formal mechanism to hear from their people. These seasons of silence present real challenges for leaders; they are literally flying blind. Listening, both through formal and informal channels, needs a much more frequent cadence to guide leadership decisions and interventions.

Limited listening mechanisms. One size does not fit all when it comes to listening mechanisms. Some people will respond in a survey, while others prefer a focus group to provide their perspective. Many organizations have fallen into the trap of choosing one format or another. We'll talk later in this chapter about a few options, but for now, all I'll say is the best organizations do both quantitative and qualitative research, often in tandem. They serve different purposes and can be used to strengthen each other.

Information overload. A final reason why listening is challenging is the overwhelming mountain of information from multiple sources an organization can amass. How do you make sense of all the input? This is no trivial question. To have data is step one, but it's not the goal. The data must be turned into insight and then into action. Many leaders are not capable of doing this work themselves, and you could even make the case they shouldn't be doing this work, anyway. This is why you see a growing trend in the field of people analytics. Someone has to make sense of the data before leaders can make the appropriate Adaptations to the culture.

FROM THE ASHES

In the aftermath of World War II, Japan was in ruins. Like many of its counterparts, its automobile industry was in shambles, crippled by the destruction of critical infrastructure and low demand. Toyota almost went bankrupt in 1949. In 1950, its production was limited to just three hundred vehicles. Back then, Japanese carmakers were known mainly for their habit of ripping off designs from other manufacturers. Toyota's first passenger car, the 1936 Model AA, was a blatant copy of Dodge and Chevrolet designs, and some of its parts could actually be interchanged with the original American ones.[2]

In an attempt to help Japan rebuild, many nations sent experts. None were more consequential than W. Edwards Deming, a professor of statistics at New York University. Deming made his first trip to Japan in 1950 to conduct a business seminar. As his concepts began to take root, Deming's status continued to rise—along with the quality of goods made in Japan. His early idea to use statistics to monitor and improve quality, combined with later refinements, became what we know today as the Toyota Production System (TPS).[3]

Although the heart of the TPS is the data, a less discussed component is the idea of listening to the people closest to the work.

My favorite example of this is embodied in the idea of *kaizen*, a Japanese word that means "change for the better" or "continuous improvement." The magic in this concept is not in the magnitude of an initial idea for improvement; it is in the cumulative effect of many small, even incremental, ideas. Any idea that could save even a few seconds is entertained. The eventual effect of these small, seemingly insignificant changes can be tremendous. In his book, *40 years, 20 Million Ideas*, Yuzo Yasuda tells the whole story of how in a typical year Toyota receives one million ideas from its employees—and a few years ago, it received over three million.[4]

This form of listening has enabled Toyota to be a global leader in the car industry.[5] With Toyota as a benchmark, how well are you listening to your employees? How many ideas are waiting to be discovered? What could you do to encourage more new ideas and suggestions from your employees? How well are you listening to them today?

DISCOVERY JOURNEY

The name LEGO is derived from two Danish words that translate to "play well." Today, the company bearing the name is a global brand with a sterling reputation. Its name captures the essence of its Aspiration—to inspire imagination, creativity, and fine motor skills. Its logo can be found on movie screens, theme parks, a hotel chain, and in the hands of children everywhere.

However, in 1998, the brand was in trouble. It posted its first significant losses in four of the seven years between 1998 and 2004. This was uncharted territory for the brand, founded in 1932. Industry shifts in the 1990s—such as toy discounters overtaking mom-and-pops, declining birth rates, and a shift toward toys that offered instant gratification—caught LEGO flatfooted. Sales dropped 30 percent in 2003 and 10 percent more in 2004.[6]

Danish turnaround expert Poul Plougmann was first tasked with reviving the company. But the by-the-book nature of his "Fitness Plan" failed to reignite the company, despite short-term cost cutting. By 2003, LEGO was virtually out of cash and had lost $300 million. The case for change was abundantly clear: LEGO needed a tailored approach for the future that would connect the heart of the company to its foundation and strength.

In 2004, the company appointed a new CEO, Jørgen Vig Knudstorp. After some cost-saving measures of his own, such as selling a major share of the company's theme park, LEGO-LAND, and moving a majority of manufacturing to Mexico and the Czech Republic, he embarked on a "discovery journey" to build a deeper understanding of LEGO's value proposition and what made the brand and the organization unique. This decision to listen and learn would prove to be transformational.[7]

Knudstorp sought input from a broad range of stakeholders—visiting retailers to understand their needs, working with MIT to understand how children learn, spending time with loyal LEGO fans at a conference, and observing how kids actually play with LEGOs. His focus was not on selling his vision or on his ideas for improvement. He was truly listening—and people were willing to talk.

Internal conversations uncovered a mismatch between what LEGO's designers were producing and what customers valued. Ethnographic studies revealed insights such as kids' delight in being challenged and how to better connect with girls through greater levels of detail and realism. Through his immersion, Knudstorp reaffirmed LEGO was more than the plastic brick. The brand stirs nostalgia, fuels learning, and sparks creativity in kids.

Realizing the company had strayed too far from its roots, Knudstorp refined the company mission to "Inspire and develop the builders of tomorrow" and charted a path to reconnect the organization with "the creative expression of the core product."[8]

With the mission and path forward clarified, Knudstorp optimized supply chain, development, and distribution to allow the company to focus on innovating with purpose once again. Knudstorp's work was immensely successful, with revenue increasing fivefold between 2005 and today—and with no signs of slowing down.[9]

FRONTLINE REALITY

A common challenge many organizations face is the disconnect between the corporate staff and the offices or outlets around the country or the globe. Far too often, frontline staff believe the people in the office are out of touch with the day-to-day realities in the field. Corporate staff are sometimes said to work in the ivory tower, a place far removed from the real world. Sadly, there is often truth in this suspicion. Fortunately, there are ways to close this reality gap.

RaceTrac, a Georgia-based company operating gasoline service stations, with over 550 locations across the southeast region of the United States, has grown tremendously; its 2021 annual sales surpassed $9 billion.[10] One of the ways it has attempted to first understand and then bridge the gap between corporate and its locations is by employing a different listening mechanism: immersion. Every year, each senior leader, vice president and above, works one week in a RaceTrac service station.

I've experienced the benefits of going to the field myself over the years, they include:

Staying grounded in reality. As a guy who has spent four decades in a corporate office, I can testify that maintaining a grasp on reality is challenging. We have been reminding our staff for many years: "Our business is *not* at the headquarters—the customers are in the restaurants." Our founder would often remind us, "There are no cash registers at the home office." Going to the field, and not just for a drop-in visit but to work for an extended amount of time, is genius. This helps leaders maintain a greater sense of what is really happening.

Gaining frontline perspective. How does it feel to interact with a disgruntled customer? What is it like to have to work an extra shift because two people have called in sick? What emotions do you experience when your IT infrastructure shuts down and you are trying to get support from your corporate helpline? Again, there is no substitute for personally experiencing these things. A PowerPoint slide about the situation is always a shallow substitute for seeing for yourself.

Increasing their visibility. One of the complaints many frontline and junior-level employees raise from time to time is the lack of visibility of senior leaders. Who are they? What's their story? What do they believe? Do they care about me? Many of these questions can be answered with a concentrated effort to put leaders in the field. There will be a ripple effect; your visit will likely echo far beyond the location you visit.

Identifying opportunity. What are the real issues in your organization? What are the obstacles to continued success? What questions and concerns do the people closest to the work have? What ideas are your employees willing to share that might never make it through the gauntlet of checks, balances, and approvals back at corporate? Many leaders will find time in the field to be extremely helpful for answering these questions and more.

Peter Drucker, the late management and leadership guru, said, "Unless [decision makers] build their feedback around direct exposure to reality—unless they discipline themselves to go out and look—they condemn themselves to a sterile dogmatism."[11] Apparently, RaceTrac agrees.

SUPERQUINN

Although I wrote about Superquinn in *Smart Leadership*, I could not omit it from this conversation about listening—specifically, listening to customers as a rich source of input as you Adapt to better fulfill your Aspiration. Superquinn was a supermarket chain founded in 1960 by Feargal Quinn. I met Feargal probably thirty years ago at a conference in San Diego and was immediately impressed with his passion for listening—so much so that I went for a visit to his home in Ireland to see for myself and learn from a master.

Quinn had a firm grip on his Aspiration. He wanted to create a store people loved. He spent many days every month walking through one of his thirty establishments, meeting his customers and asking them for ideas to improve their shopping experience. Because he was an early adopter of shopper cards, he had access to customers' home addresses. After meeting someone, he would often jot down their name and then later check his database to retrieve their address. He sent countless handwritten notes thanking customers for their business and, reflecting on their brief encounter in the store, would often acknowledge the specific suggestion or idea they had shared with him.

Although this was clearly over-the-top behavior for the CEO of a large organization, Quinn didn't consider all this one-on-one contact sufficient. Once a week, Quinn would personally conduct a focus group with customers—once a week! It's hard to imagine he could invest so much of his time with customers, but he found extreme value in meeting with, listening to, and learning from them. They informed the Adaptations he needed to make to fulfill his Aspirations for the culture he was trying to create.

LISTEN TO UNDERSTAND

As I have already alluded to, there are many ways leaders can listen. And although Quinn is an extreme example, I know other leaders who also participate in focus groups (though on a less frequent basis). My team and I use them as well. If you've not observed or led a formal focus group, why not give it a try? Here are a few tips to help you get started.

Who do I talk to? Which group of people can help you better understand the realities of your culture? Here are a few ideas:

- Employees at different levels within the organization
- Employees with more than ten years of experience
- Employees who have worked in your organization for less than two years
- Employees who all do the same job
- Employees who have left your company

I know one senior leader who likes to meet with young employees on a regular basis. Say what you will about young people entering the workforce, but I believe they are some of the most inspired workers I have ever met. However, they do see the world differently. This is not bad, but it can create real challenges for leaders who do not understand their worldview. You can take steps to bridge these cultural and generational gaps if you invest the time to listen.

What topics should I explore? What topics would you like to explore? A meet and greet is fine, but you can do more and learn more. Depending on the group assembled and what issues you want to explore, you can learn a lot about your culture and potential opportunities for Adaptation (that is, improvement) by asking the right questions. These might include:

- Which part of our culture was most appealing to you before you joined the company, and why? Have your hopes been fulfilled? If not, what could we do to better align our promise with our practices?
- What examples have you seen of us living out our purpose? Where are we falling short?
- Which of our values do you see most consistently demonstrated? Which ones do we need to work on?

- What behaviors do you observe that seem inconsistent with the culture we are trying to create?
- What suggestions do you have to strengthen our culture?

This list could go on and on. The point is to ask strong, open-ended questions and listen. Only then can you make thoughtful and informed changes to your culture. (If you want additional questions, scan the QR code in the back of this book for a free *Culture Rules* Field Guide).

How will I respond? If you are conducting focus groups or surveys with internal audiences, keep in mind people expect to hear or see a response. If you receive input from a group of ten people, follow up with those individuals. Let them know you heard them, and if you can, provide a tangible next step—this always helps. If you cannot provide a decision on their specific ideas or suggestions, respond regardless. Let them know you're listening, and update them with the next steps you plan to take.

YOUR NEXT STEP

Your next step is to make a commitment to Adapt and continuously improve your culture. Then commit (or recommit) to listening. The strategies and tactics in your action plan matter less than your dogged determination to search for the truth about your culture and the current state of your Aspiration. You should always be monitoring the pulse of your culture.

Here are just some of the things you want to be listening for: What is working? What is not working? What, if anything, is creating mixed messages about your Aspiration? Is your Aspiration still relevant? Is it understood? What would make the

Aspiration clearer for your various stakeholder groups—employees, vendors, board members, and customers? How could you enhance the buy-in of all audiences?

Remember, the truth is often hiding in plain sight. As I wrote in *Smart Leadership*, "Although our reality is all around us, [the truth] isn't always obvious—it often lurks in disguise, evading our casual glances. And it always shuns our half-hearted efforts to expose it." Leave no stone unturned.

YOUR MOVE...

If you wanted to secure the most accurate and complete information regarding the state of your culture, what would you need to do?

MEASURE WHAT MATTERS

Measurement is fabulous. Unless you're busy measuring what's easy to measure as opposed to what's important.
—**Seth Godin**

As we conducted our research, the question of measurement was one of the most interesting areas of exploration. We talked to scores of leaders about the topic. We discovered their opinions on measurement were all over the game board.

Some thought the measurement of culture impossible. These people were in the "culture is invisible, like the wind" category. Obviously, they have never heard of an anemometer—an instrument for measuring the speed and direction of the wind.

Others were in the "it's really hard to measure culture" category. These leaders and their organizations failed to embrace the significance of a thriving culture. Their busyness had distracted them, even blinded them, to the long-term health implications of not pursuing any metrics for their culture.

And some were laser-focused on the power and necessity of measuring culture. This group was in the minority but was generally of the mindset that "to have no measure of your cultural health, vitality, and efficacy would be like attempting to lead your business without a profit and loss statement."

There were leaders all along this continuum, including some in the middle, whose measures of cultural health were based on intuition and experience. I would not doubt these leaders. I have known leaders with a sixth sense about their organizations. This is fabulous for them, but it is not scalable.

So, where did the team and I net out on this? We'll get to our conclusion in a moment. But first, let's consider why a leader might not want to measure the state of their organization's culture.

The Aspiration is not clear. If you don't know what you are trying to create, any exercise in measurement will be an exercise in frustration and futility.

The truth hurts. The leaders may have assessed their culture before and didn't like what they discovered. The best leaders confront reality; they don't cower in its presence. Like an undiagnosed cancer, a toxic culture can metastasize and destroy the entire enterprise.

Priorities keep changing. Many organizations struggle with focus. If leaders continue to change their Aspiration, strategies, and tactics, knowing what to measure can become very difficult.

Ignorance is bliss. I know of leaders who found the cultural changes they desired exceedingly difficult to execute. Therefore, every time their organizations would assess the culture, the leaders' "report cards" would not improve. The response: "Let's stop measuring culture."

They'd rather just wing it. There are probably deep psychological and personality issues at play here, which I am not qualified to address. However, as I mentioned previously, relying on just one person who has the power of discernment is not scalable.

Before we look at a few organizations that have overcome these obstacles, I want to acknowledge that I am not aware of any perfect metric or set of metrics for unilaterally measuring culture. I will say, though, the ones appearing to serve their organizations best are built to align as much as possible with the specific Aspiration the leaders have articulated and Amplified.

WHY MEASURE CULTURE?

If I were leading an organization, I would make every effort to measure the strength of the culture. I would employ a combination of qualitative and quantitative methods. The only exemption I can imagine would be if the organization were very small. If this is your situation, perhaps proactive and regular listening sessions alone will suffice. As soon as you cannot know with confidence how every employee is connecting to the Aspiration and striving to make it a reality, I would add some form of formal measurement. The benefits of measurement include the following.

Enables you to Adapt wisely. There are numerous reasons to measure culture, but the ability to Adapt thoughtfully, strategically, and wisely is first among equals. Remember, the third rule is to always work to enhance your culture. Without measurement, you are like a pilot flying without any instruments. It is possible, but the risk of calamity increases significantly. Of the countless opportunities before you, where should you invest your time, energy, and resources? Are there any raging fires to address? Are there smoldering issues you could address before they become a wildfire? Are there strengths in your culture you want to leverage and celebrate? Measurement is the key to unlocking these questions and more.

Allows you to quantify the health of your culture. There are a number of parallels between culture and the world of physical health. The United Health Foundation compiles an index of data derived from four categories: social and economic factors, physical environment, clinical care, and behaviors—all of which contribute to predictable health outcomes. Blue Cross Blue Shield has an index calculated from over forty million individuals with more than three hundred diagnostic questions.[1]

Thankfully, you don't need anything nearly this elaborate to quantify the health of your culture—but you can build a system to determine how aligned your organization is, or is not, on things that matter. Knowing this type of information could be a game changer. Your degree of alignment on these critical issues is the strength of your culture.

Can help you spot trends. If you establish a measurement process and cadence, you will be able to spot and monitor trends over time. This also allows you to validate strategies for improvement and to redirect if your efforts are not working. I have experienced this firsthand. When the same issue surfaces in survey after survey, the countermeasures you are using aren't working.

Sends a signal to your organization. Establishing a formal process for measuring the strength of your culture sends a strong signal to the entire organization that you really do care about this topic. Whereas, if you don't measure it, people could misinterpret this as a lack of care, urgency, or priority. Remember, people always watch the leader and the projects you support.

Creates an early warning system. There are toxins lurking in every organization. Needless to say, they are not good. What makes them so insidious is they are often unseen . . . until it is too late. Measurement can give you a heads-up and a head start as you begin taking appropriate actions. If you are attentive, you may be able to address concerns before they are widespread.

Vibrant cultures use measurement to assess the degree of alignment between their Aspiration and their reality. When there is a gap, they Adapt.

THE ANSWER IS...

Let's assume for a moment you buy into the importance of formal measurement. I often receive questions from leaders who want to know which tool or assessment I would recommend. My answer may surprise you.

Even though I am a huge advocate for measuring organizational culture, I am a huge skeptic when it comes to off-the-shelf solutions. If you go all the way back to the beginning of this book, you'll find I wrote about the uniqueness of every culture. This glorious attribute makes one-size-fits-all measurement solutions dubious at best. The exception would be if your Aspiration aligns with someone else's point of view, such as Microsoft's focus on a growth mindset. Since Carol Dweck and her team at Stanford already pioneered the work on growth mindsets, Microsoft can just use Dweck's assessment. If you can't find an off-the-shelf solution that allows you to assess your specific Aspiration, you'll need to build your own culture scorecard and measurement system.

What is *your* Aspiration? What are *your* values? What is *your* purpose? I would strongly suggest you probe these items and others like them. Then, and only then, will you know what you need to measure to inform your efforts to Adapt. Only when you Adapt wisely can you enhance the health of your culture and increase the success of your organization. Let's look at how some organizations think about measuring the health of their culture.

Lee Company

Not all measurement has to be big and comprehensive. There is a growing trend in short, simple, and typically more frequent "pulse surveys." In some cases, the questions in a pulse survey change with each round, and in other cases, the questions remain constant.

Lee Company is a family-owned organization offering services such as HVAC, plumbing, electrical, and appliance repair to large construction projects. It has been using its Workday platform to distribute weekly pulse surveys to its almost 1,500 employees (this is in addition to its annual survey).

The weekly surveys ask three simple questions:

1. How did your week go?
2. Do you feel like your manager cares?
3. Do you feel like you did something that made an impact in the organization?

I ran an experiment a couple of years ago in about thirty of our restaurants with this pulse-survey idea. Our platform was an app. At the end of each shift, team members were asked no more than three questions. Over the course of the project, we used several different questions for our survey.

The question team members were most excited about was this: How did you help someone win today? In just a couple of months, a pool of about 2,500 employees had submitted more than forty thousand responses to this single question. We learned a lot by reviewing the individual responses, and many of the restaurants reported a transformation in their cultures just from asking the question. Pulse surveys can be powerful.

Southwest Airlines

Southwest Airlines does a lot of things exceptionally well. I have personally benchmarked with the organization on multiple occasions over many years. Topics have ranged from creating a leadership culture to improving execution. We have hosted its leaders in Atlanta, and I have visited with them in Dallas. They continue to work to create one of the world's great organizations.

The Southwest Airlines leadership fundamentally believes caring for employees will translate to better customer service and experiences. In an industry focused on operations, the company uses metrics to track the health of its culture, indicated by employee quarterly pulse surveys. These surveys track employees' development opportunities and sentiments. The information is compiled and reported in quarterly reviews leaders use to prioritize areas for improvement and create an action plan.

Given the regular cadence of collecting feedback, leaders have clear trends to track over time. One of their top priorities is to build a culture focused on employee happiness and well-being.

Qualtrics

Qualtrics is an experience management company, so it stands to reason it would want its employees to have an outstanding work experience. The cultural metric it has chosen as its focus is employee engagement. Qualtrics believes this measure will both drive growth and enable it to assess the effectiveness of its leaders.

During one of our interviews for this project, a Qualtrics leader told us about their belief in the centrality of engagement.

> One of the key missions of the company is to have the highest possible engagement score for every people leader and their respective team. If the scores are not where they should be, our Chief People Officer will sit down with the leader and help them create a tangible action plan to fix it. We believe engagement is essential to maintaining our leadership position and sustaining growth.[2]

Let's talk about engagement as a measure of culture. Qualtrics is not the only organization using engagement as a proxy for cultural health. REI; Verizon; Mars, Inc.; Nationwide; and many others have also adopted this as the primary or singular metric. My take on this is to simply be careful. If, like Microsoft and its focus on a growth mindset, your entire Aspiration for your culture can be distilled to engagement, then go for it. But my fear is that selecting engagement is often a shortcut and substitute for what could be a more helpful and robust measure or set of metrics.

On more than one occasion, I have talked to leaders who are frustrated with the promise of engagement. There is an almost mystical belief that a high level of engagement will solve all of an organization's problems. It will not.

I remember one leader who confided in me her people were fully engaged, and she even went a step further and said her team had created a great place to work that was fun and energizing for all employees. The employees loved the leader and their teammates. As she continued to describe her organization, she concluded with the admission there was only one problem: "The team's performance is awful."

We don't have time to fully diagnose this leader's situation. She may have been correct about her team's high level of engagement. Yet, as I told her, she may have lost sight of the goal; engagement is *not* the goal—it is part of a much bigger picture. Go back to the definition of a High Performance Culture from "Before You Play." It includes "superior levels of performance over time."

You get to decide what is important in your culture, and as I just said, I think engagement matters! I even wrote an entire book on the topic. However, I think assuming a direct causal relationship between engagement and performance is risky at best. You can be fully engaged in your local country club, church, or civic group, but that has no bearing on whether any of those organizations have built a High Performance Culture.

I think you should care about engagement and *more*. You should care about how people are led and the level of alignment within your organization. And you should really care about *what* people are aligned to (i.e., your vision and values). Be careful you don't sell your organization and your culture short with a narrow and incomplete Aspiration. Engagement is essential but insufficient.

APPEARANCES CAN BE DECEIVING

Have you ever known anyone who was sick and didn't know it? I have, and in a few of those cases, it didn't end well. By the time they were diagnosed, it was too late. If a person looks fine and feels great, they may still be sick. Potentially really sick. The same can be true for an organization.

I am sure many employees at Wells Fargo were unaware of the toxicity gaining strength in their organization as millions of false accounts were opened to reach quotas and sales goals. Enron was lauded year after year for its innovation, including the year it went out of business. Appearances can be deceiving.

A few years ago, I went for my first physical. Given the way my day at the clinic was organized, I would need to move from one building to another and back to complete the assessment. The staff arranged for a golf cart with a driver to move me across their campus.

My driver was full of life; he was enthusiastic and cheerful. He had a welcoming spirit and a warm smile that offered a nice break between the rigors of the various tests. He told me one of the perks of working at the clinic was a free physical. When he went through one such assessment, he learned he had life-threatening cancer. He'd had no idea! He received treatment and survived. "This job saved my life," he said. "I'm glad you are getting a physical today. I hope all goes well."

When you and your organization decide to pursue some form of cultural assessment or formal measurement, if you do find an issue, you can respond accordingly. You may not have a terminal case—I hope you do not! Early detection, however, is often the key to a cure.

YOUR MOVE...

How are you measuring the health of your culture?

DON'T BREATHE

He who creates a poison also has the cure.
—Suzy Kassem

I n the late 1800s, the developed world was booming and the Second Industrial Revolution was gaining momentum. Many know the names Thomas Edison, Henry Ford, and Cornelius Vanderbilt; their creativity and leadership are a matter of history. However, the unsung heroes of this era were those who harvested the fuel for the industrial engine.

During this time, coal was the predominant source of energy in America, having recently surpassed wood for this distinction.[1] Coal lacked the luster of gold and the brilliance of diamonds, yet it was the silent partner bankrolling the progress the world enjoyed.

Increasing demand created increasing pressure on the mining industry. As a result, it was not uncommon for men to work long, back-breaking shifts, spending countless hours in cold, treacherous, and dimly lit conditions to extract the dark treasure from the earth.

The only thing darker than the mines themselves was the

thought of their nemesis: poisonous gases, including methane, hydrogen sulfide, and the odorless, tasteless, and toxic carbon monoxide. Many workers lost their lives at the hands of this silent killer. Working one minute; overcome the next. Once you succumbed to the gas, survival was unlikely.[2]

Aware of the dangers, miners tried many techniques to detect the deadly gases. One of the more brazen was the human wick.

Prior to beginning a shift, a worker covered in a wet blanket would enter the caves carrying a long, lighted wick. He would move the flame around the edges of the ceiling and the walls. If gas was present in smaller quantities, there would be a flare-up but nothing catastrophic. However, if the intrepid miner encountered a large pocket of gas, he might not survive.[3]

In 1911, after fifteen years of study and experimentation, Dr. John Scott Haldane had an idea. His solution was to send canaries into the mine with the men. A canary? What could this delicate, beautiful, and tiny bird possibly have to offer the courageous men who worked in the mines? Life.

But why a canary? The answer is found in the bird's anatomy. To be able to fly as high as they do, canaries have lungs that are engineered to intake oxygen when they inhale *and* exhale. This level of oxygen saturation combined with their small size makes them hyper-sensitive to poisonous gases.[4]

You may know the rest of the story: men began carrying the birds with them into the mines, and if the birds passed out or became sick, often signaled by less chirping, the men knew to evacuate. Thus, the saying "canary in a coal mine" was born to represent an early warning signal for impending danger.

The connection between this story and the promise of this

book may not be obvious at first glance. Please allow me to connect a few dots.

Just like the gases that plagued the miners, culture is invisible. It is the sum of many influences. We can see the manifestation of these forces culminating in culture, but often we cannot see the root.

The hiddenness of toxins in the mines did not minimize their impact on the workers. Nor does your inability to see culture minimize its significance. Just like the air the miners breathed, the culture your organization attempts to work in has significant ramifications on the health, vitality, and even survival of your organization.

When the culture is vibrant, it is like pure oxygen to those who work there. However, when a culture becomes toxic, it can make an organization very sick . . . or even kill it.

The early-warning systems modern leaders create are much more complicated than Haldane's canaries, as they should be. Many of the organizations in our world are large, bureaucratic, and plagued by personal and political agendas, and some are divided by time zones and even continents. As outlined in the previous chapters, wise leaders create systems capable of identifying the harbingers of organizational illness while it is still contained and before it becomes a raging pandemic. Experienced leaders understand that what begins as malaise can quickly become a terminal condition.

The World Health Organization publishes the International Classification of Diseases (ICD). Its most recent release, the ICD-11, includes around 55,000 unique codes for injuries, diseases, and causes of death.[5] How many different codes would we need to catalog all the maladies impacting the modern workplace? Hard to say.

How does the healthcare profession wrap its head around 55,000 injuries, diseases, and causes of death? Well, in part, human diseases can be divided into four categories—infectious diseases, deficiency diseases, hereditary diseases, and physiological diseases. We'll see if similar categorization can help you protect your organization (so you don't have to buy a canary).

This chapter will not only help you prepare for these pathogens, it will also give you a shared language. This is one of the many benefits of the ICD; healthcare workers around the globe can speak a common language as they work to improve the health of the planet. I trust that identifying and labeling these maladies and sharing their primary causes will enable you and your leaders to have more productive conversations as you create your plans to eradicate the issues encumbering your organization and prevent future outbreaks.

Obviously, this chapter will not call out all the toxins you can find in modern organizations or all the ill effects they can create if left unchecked. It does, however, attempt to catalog the most prevalent ones in order to give you a head start at diagnosing them in your organization.

I have divided this chapter into two sections: "Something in the Air" and "Modern Maladies." Together, these sections give face and form to some of the forces at play within many organizations.

A final word before we jump in: there are no perfect organizations. Some molecules of the toxins we are about to review likely live in every organization. Our job as leaders is to stand vigilant and respond. We are the primary guardians of the culture. What may be an isolated incident can become a raging outbreak if left unchecked.

What do you do when you discover these agents of impending dysfunction? We'll answer this question in the next chapter. For now, let's see what we are up against.

SOMETHING IN THE AIR

Just like we know asbestos, mercury, and lead can cause cancer, we know some of the agents wreaking havoc in our modern organizations. As we completed our research for this project, we made a list of the most common ones we encountered.

Indifference. Indifference is one of the primary signs of trouble for organizations around the world. A common metric used to discern this is engagement. In essence, engagement is a reflection of how much people care about their work, their coworkers, and their organization. According to ADP's most recent global survey, the number of people fully engaged at work is a miserable 16 percent.[6] The untapped potential resident in these workers is beyond my comprehension. This is not a problem with the workforce; this is a problem with the culture of these organizations. Therefore, this is a leadership problem, and perhaps the greatest leadership opportunity ever to exist on a global scale.

Paranoia. You may have experienced or witnessed paranoia before—if so, hopefully only in isolated cases. This toxin is rooted in self-preservation and the mindset "I had better watch my back." When this attitude is prevalent, it will manifest in the tendency for people to care more about themselves than about their colleagues or their organization. Behaviors often associated with this attitude are lack of collaboration, a reluctance to present new ideas (for fear someone else will take credit), and a tendency to be self-promoting. The sources of this toxin could be numerous, including past wrongs, real or perceived, or a lack of confidence or trust in leadership to do the right thing.

Mistrust. The source of mistrust can be hard to pinpoint—it can seep into an organization from many places. If the leader is the one people do not trust, you can begin to explore questions about their character. Do they walk the talk? Do they have the moral authority to lead? Assuming you find no major character issues, the next place to turn is competency. Does the leader know how to lead? Have they actually demonstrated leadership in the past? If not, this could create a trust gap. Another source of mistrust is a leader with fleeting interests: a leader constantly shifting the organization's focus without finishing the previous "priority." This behavior has other consequences as well—see the section on whiplash below.

If the mistrust appears to be more peer-to-peer, I would argue the leader is still responsible. They must be aware of the situation and intervene to restore trust between their colleagues.

Deafness. When leaders don't listen, you can expect virtually any situation to worsen. People want to be heard. They want their opinions to at least be considered. Employees want to be valued for their heads and not just their hands. When leaders are overconfident or lacking in humility, a natural and predictable outcome is an unwillingness to listen. If this condition persists, people will stop talking. The only voices the leader will hear are those who wholeheartedly support their ideas. This creates an echo chamber, which is perhaps the most dangerous place to lead from.

Whiplash. In the modern organization, there are many teams, projects, and initiatives underway at any given time. This is to be expected. A successful organization can successfully juggle many balls at once. However, individuals do not have the same capacity for multitasking as the organization at large. Whiplash is what happens when an individual employee or team is constantly being pulled and torn in different directions. One factor that can exacerbate this is high leadership turnover. Each new leader brings their own agenda, complete with urgent priorities and impending deadlines.

Leaders should be the ultimate arbiters regarding which work an individual or team should tackle at any given time. Otherwise, unfocused busyness and constant change can become toxic.

Disingenuousness. Candor is core to creating a healthy culture. But in many workplaces, being open and honest is not welcomed. If this critical success factor is missing, it is often replaced by excessive politeness. We interviewed a leader from a multibillion-dollar organization who said, in essence, that what is valued in her organization is niceness and agreeability, not truth.

In our attempt to help leaders improve their effectiveness, one of the things we learned and wrote about in *Smart Leadership* is that the best leaders choose to Confront Reality. Only when they do can they stay grounded in truth and lead from a place of strength. If you are allowing politeness to overtake candor as the norm, your leadership impact will be compromised, and it will be exceedingly difficult for your organization to thrive.

Countercultures. One of the findings from our research was the existence of microcultures in every organization. This really wasn't much of a finding; of course organizations have microcultures. Accounting departments will always be different from marketing departments, and the research and development folks are different from both. This is not bad. This becomes toxic, however, when these microcultures morph into countercultures.

Countercultures work *against* the norms, values, and purpose of the organization at large. They are a cancer in the larger body of the organization. Left unchecked, they will infuse negative values into the company and undermine productivity and leadership.

Self-deception. Is your organization honest with itself? Do your leaders and your employees assume ownership of your gaps and opportunities? Or have you achieved enough success and acclaim that you are tempted to hide the truth? Do you value people who ask hard questions? Do you recognize those who bring facts to the table? Too many leaders are reading their own press clippings. They are blinded by their own optimism. They cannot see the future because they do not have an honest appraisal of the present. A better tomorrow always begins with a clear assessment of today. Drivers of self-deceptive behavior can include hubris, an overly optimistic worldview, fear, or a misplaced belief in the future being an extension of the past.

MODERN MALADIES

Unlike the World Health Organization, we cannot begin to list all the permutations of modern organizational maladies. Therefore, we have identified six broad types of maladies to classify the extreme cases in which leaders do not sufficiently purge toxins.

I choose the word "maladies" because these conditions are not innocuous like the common cold. If they were, they would be little more than an inconvenience; unfortunately, at the stage we'll describe here, they are deep-seated and chronic. In some cases, they may even be terminal. Even if they are not fatal, they always create drag in an organization and are at war with your Aspiration. The goal of the leadership should be to eliminate these forms of behavior from the culture whenever possible.

Members Only. This is a culture in which decision-making is largely centralized, at least on issues of significance. Input may be tolerated but is not welcomed. The conversations leading to decisions are typically held behind closed doors. The logic and rationale for decisions is rarely shared. Often in these situations, there is low trust and confidence in leadership.

Employees at Uber experienced a form of this culture type: senior leadership rewarded the wrong employees, permitted poor behaviors, and more. The consequences were far-reaching. In 2017, Uber's CEO, Travis Kalanick, stepped down due to charges of sexual harassment—and this was only a surface-level sign of deeper cultural issues.

After Kalanick's departure, Uber launched an internal investigation, and the information it received was stunning. Hundreds of allegations ranging from sexual harassment, discrimination, bullying, retaliation, and more had been filed, yet many of those allegations had long been unaddressed by the organization. This led to twenty employees being fired.[7]

There are several fundamental problems with this type of culture. One is the chokehold leaders have on ideas, debate, and dissent. Without productive conflict, no organization can reach its full potential.

Hopefully, you have no firsthand experience with a culture suffering under a "members only" diagnosis. If you do, I hope the CEO and other senior leaders adopted their highly autocratic methods without nefarious intent. Unfortunately, many of the outcomes will be the same regardless of motives.

The Untouchables. The predominant vibe from these cultures is somewhere between arrogance and hubris. These are the organizations that believe they can do no wrong. They may think they are too big or too smart to fail; nonetheless, they eventually pay the price for their misguided confidence. The *Titanic* was the "unsinkable ship."

Consider the case of Lehman Brothers. Founded in 1850, the organization had a long history of customer service and value creation. It took pride in the partnerships it built with clients, and its growth and profitability came as a result of these relationships.

After Bobbie Lehman died in 1969, the culture began to change. The new leadership built increasingly lucrative pay-for-performance bonus systems for their employees. Over the next twenty years, the role of customers slowly changed. They came to be considered a means to an end: profits and bonuses. In 2008, the leadership of new CEO Richard Fuld intensified the pressure to grow at all costs. In September of 2008, Lehman Brothers filed for bankruptcy, the largest in US history at the time, involving more than $600 billion in assets.[8]

The Gladiators. You may not know of this type of culture personally, but you have certainly heard about it in the news. It can best be characterized as a "survival of the fittest" culture. In such cultures, there is often an undercurrent of paranoia that engulfs the organization. Who will win? Who will lose? As a result, ideas are hoarded, and everyone loses.

A classic example of this "gladiator" malady is Enron. For those not familiar with Enron's story, Enron was a highly regarded energy and trading company founded in 1985 by Kenneth Lay. The company was heralded as the most innovative company in America for six consecutive years by *Fortune* magazine, and the *Financial Times* awarded Enron the "Energy Company of the Year" in 2000.[9] But all that glitters is not gold.

Behind closed doors, the culture was known for its cutthroat performance evaluation procedures. The Performance Review Committee (PRC) was often referred to within the company as "rank and yank."

Deal makers were rewarded handsomely but only for closing deals; there was no evaluation regarding whether the deal was good for the organization overall. Also, the compensation system paid upon closing, with no consideration of the long-term viability or sustainability of the relationship. As a result, customer service was not a priority.

Because an employee's annual bonuses (as well as promotions, future job opportunities within the company, or even continued employment) were determined by PRC rankings, managers fought mightily to promote and protect their favorite employees.

All of this and several other factors, including some dubious accounting practices, proved too much for the company to overcome. On December 2, 2001, Enron declared bankruptcy, the largest in history at that time. Its shareholders lost over $50 billion in value.[10]

Hive Mind. This culture is often caught in a time warp. Often, these organizations' successes were in the past, and no one realizes the world has changed. The culture is characterized by a lack of new ideas, and if any show up, they are not welcomed. Blind compliance and consensus are the priorities. A sense of heritage and legacy becomes the touchstone even as the world changes around them.

This is an apt description of where IBM was in the '70s and '80s. At the time, IBM was the largest computer company in the world—and maybe the smartest. It invested tremendous sums of money into research and development, and in 1986, two of its team members won the Nobel Prize in physics. The organization felt it was invincible largely due to the caliber of its people. Above all, it prided itself on a culture of innovation.

The problem: this historical and idealized IBM no longer existed. The "wild ducks" it prided itself on hiring had all been shot. The innovators were gone; they could not survive in the new IBM, which was bureaucratic, slow, and unlikely to change. IBM had grown a culture of conformity, with leaders who were slowly overseeing the death of a once great organization. By the early 1990s, IBM was on the brink of bankruptcy. Enter Lou Gerstner, who over the next five years revived the sleeping giant by focusing on changing the culture.

Big Brother. All the maladies we are discussing are the by-products of the toxins we discussed previously in various mixtures. The tipping point is when these toxins overwhelm the culture and become the prevailing attribute of the culture. When this happens, the symptoms are easily recognizable. When Big Brother takes hold, low engagement is often a contributing factor and a telltale sign.

In these environments, leaders must closely monitor the activities of their teams. Employees are viewed as cogs in the machine—as replaceable parts. Value must be extracted from the workforce. Complacency is a common attitude among employees. Prolonged low engagement leads to apathy, stagnation, and turnover. These beliefs have deep roots, going back more than one hundred years.

The year was 1911, and Frederick Taylor had just published his book *The Principles of Scientific Management.* He was a mechanical engineer by training and turned his attention to improving industrial efficiency. The Second Industrial Revolution was gaining steam, and organizations everywhere were interested in Taylor's new methods.

For hundreds of years, there had been no increase in the ability of workers to produce or move goods. When Taylor started propounding his principles, nine out of every ten working people did manual work, whether in manufacturing, farming, mining, or transportation.[11]

Prior to Taylor, work was largely controlled by the worker. In those days, unions were craft monopolies requiring five- to seven-year apprenticeships. Scientific management, however, changed all of this. Taylor put all the responsibility for getting work done on management. As some have said about the heart of Taylorism, "Leaders think, supervisors talk, and workers work." The implications of this philosophy still haunt the world today.

House of Cards. As the story goes, two swindlers came to town and discovered a king who invested vast amounts of money on his wardrobe. The men convinced the king they could provide him with a suit with mystical properties. The clothes would be invisible to all those who were stupid or incompetent; everyone else would see their magnificence and beauty. The king bought the tale and the invisible clothes. None of his advisors wished to tell the king the truth for fear of his response. The truth was only revealed during a processional in the public square when a young boy commented, "The king has no clothes."

If this story feels all too familiar to you, you may have encountered a culture based on deception—a house of cards. Self-deception, denial, and dishonesty are all potential fuel sources for this culture. Values are professed and not lived. There is an air of invincibility permeating the culture until its last breath. Leaders of such cultures, and often their followers as well, cannot tell the difference between what is real and the narrative they have created for themselves. The house they have built is always on the verge of collapse. A recent example of this type of culture is Theranos.

In 2014, Elizabeth Holmes was changing the world—or at least she was pretending to. She was chasing an idea: What if from a single drop of blood you could conduct hundreds of lab tests? Her list included everything from cholesterol screenings to complex genetic analyses. As a result of this apparent breakthrough, her company, Theranos, took off, and Holmes became the youngest female self-made billionaire. Theranos was estimated to be worth $9 billion.[12]

Unfortunately, it all appears to have been an elaborate hoax. On January 4, 2022, a jury decided the entire scheme was a crime. Holmes was found guilty on four counts and is planning an appeal.[13] Regardless of whether her actions are ultimately deemed criminal or not, the case proves once again a culture can be overrun by deceit and deception. When these toxins invade a culture, don't breathe—run!

———

Be vigilant. Most toxins and the maladies they spawn can be detected and eliminated. Even if your organization has already begun to manifest chronic symptoms, most cultures can still survive . . . if they are well led.

YOUR MOVE...

Which of the toxins and maladies listed above are most likely to surface in your organization?

MASTER CLASS

Nothing will work unless you do.
—Maya Angelou

L et's go back to the musical defenders who provided the early detection of deadly gases for the miners working deep within the earth.

A lesser-known facet of the story are the lengths to which many miners went in order to save their feathered friends if they fell ill. Some had a small, sealed chamber, referred to as a "revival cage," for these situations. The protocol was to flood the chamber with oxygen, and often this intervention would save the bird.

You have the same opportunity. When you see early warning signs of danger, you can respond. You can save the day when people in your organization have been subjected to toxins in your culture. The interventions you undertake will help you create a workplace where the halls, literal or virtual, are filled with pure, life-giving, performance-enhancing oxygen.

YOUR TIME TO LEAD

Imagine you are the CEO of your organization (you may be; if so, this should be easy for you). You have just received your first official report on the health and well-being of your culture. The news is mixed—several facets of your culture are strong, but a few others are fairly anemic, and you see a couple of signs of serious trouble. What do you do next?

This is no trivial question. People are watching—everyone is watching. Assuming your report was informed by some type of listening mechanism, one of the implicit promises you made when you asked people to share their opinion was transparency. The organization is expecting a response.

Some of the conclusions we reached during the research for this book were driven by the data (e.g., 71 percent of leaders believe culture is their most important tool to drive performance). However, we also found our interviews to be a rich source of insight and instruction. As leaders shared their stories and experiences, a beautiful and intricate tapestry began to emerge.

When you talk to leaders about how they've responded in the face of cultural challenges, the stories are often inspiring—but at other times disheartening. I say disheartening because in many situations, leaders and their organizations are not able to turn the cultural tide and later suffer the consequences. In such cases, all that remains is the hope that the next leader will be better prepared for the cultural challenges awaiting their arrival.

In this chapter, you will be taking a master class from seven leaders who faced very different circumstances—all responding to toxins out of control. In several of these situations, the conditions had degenerated to the point where survival hung in the balance. Each leader took a different path to restore the health and vitality of their culture, some more successful than others. As you read the following section, please keep two things in mind:

1. Different situations can require drastically different responses.
2. Regardless of the countermeasures you employ, *you must do something.*

Before we explore these options, I freely admit the possible solutions to the cultural obstacles you face are infinite. Hopefully, these examples will stir your imagination to those possibilities. Now is your time to lead!

RIP THE BAND-AID

Create drastic, radical, and often painful change in a short period of time.

On January 28, 1986, the sun rose with a briskness in the air, at least by Florida standards—the temperature had dropped below freezing the night before. Liftoff had been delayed to allow the ice on the launchpad to melt. At launch, the temperature was thirty-six degrees Fahrenheit, yet the skies were clear and the crowds still gathered to watch the twenty-fifth launch of the US Space Shuttle program. What no one knew, with the exception of a few engineers, was that disaster was a real possibility.

The space shuttle *Challenger* launched as scheduled and broke apart seventy-three seconds into its flight, killing all seven crew members aboard. America was in shock. The tragedy took center stage for President Reagan. Instead of his scheduled State of the Union Address, he offered words of comfort to a grieving nation. He concluded his brief remarks with this:

> The crew of the space shuttle *Challenger* honored us by the manner in which they lived their lives. We will never forget them, nor the last time we saw them, this morning, as they prepared for their journey and waved goodbye and "slipped the surly bonds of earth" to "touch the face of God."[1]

President Reagan was not finished. He wanted our nation to learn from this tragic event. He suspended the shuttle program for thirty-two months until the completion of the Rogers Commission Report, detailing an investigation into the events leading up to the fateful morning. When its work was finished, the Rogers Commission was ultimately critical of NASA's culture and decision-making process. It revealed test data from 1977, almost a decade earlier, showing a potentially catastrophic flaw in the shuttle's O-rings, which would later lead to the *Challenger* disaster. NASA managers had also disregarded warnings from engineers about the dangers of launching in cold temperatures.

In the aftermath of the *Challenger* incident, NASA established the Office of Safety, Reliability, and Quality Assurance and instituted immediate changes in the culture and practices of the organization. This single move would forever change the culture of the organization. A series of complex checks and balances slowed virtually every aspect of the organization. With the new norms and processes in place, NASA became theoretically safer, but it has also become a bureaucracy so encumbered by fear of failure that it has now become almost impossible to innovate within it. This should serve as a sobering reminder—counter-measures effectively deployed have consequences, some antici-pated and others unintended.[2]

This "rip the Band-Aid" approach is a strategy to create dras-tic, even revolutionary change by completely and totally rewrit-ing your values, creating a new identity, or introducing radically different ways of working in a very short period of time. You will likely use this approach sparingly.

CALL YOUR SHOT
Tell people what you are going to change and why...
then do it.

In several variations of the game of pool, you must tell your op-ponent into which pocket you intend to sink the final ball. If you are successful, you win. In the world of countermeasures, sometimes a leader will explicitly call the shot regarding the cul-tural changes they are attempting to create. There is no mystery, little drama, and not much debate. The call has been made. All that remains is to see if the leader can make good on their pro-nouncement. This is the approach CEO J. Patrick Doyle took when remaking the culture, mindset, and core competency at Domino's Pizza . . . twice.

Soon after Doyle assumed the top job in 2010, the company launched a legendary campaign admitting to the world its pizza was not good. Doyle himself appeared in these ads, telling the public he would "work days, nights, and weekends" to make the pizza better. After about eighteen months of research, develop-ment, and extensive consumer testing, Doyle and his team even-tually did fix the pizza. Then Doyle turned his attention to what was arguably a much bigger challenge: the move from a pizza business to a technology company.[3]

Talk about a culture shift! What Doyle had his sights set on was not just a change in strategy; it was a cultural shift of epic proportions. He said, "Because we are in the delivery business, we have to be a technology business."[4] At the time he made this statement, half of his corporate staff was dedicated to software and analytics. What was all this technology pointing to? Customer experience and ordering options. Currently, there are fifteen different ways to order a Domino's pizza, including my personal favorite: zero-click ordering.

With the Zero Click app, you can save a favorite order. Afterward, when you open the app, your order will be placed in ten seconds unless you cancel it—all you do is wait. (If you're willing to click a few times, though, you can also track the progress of your pizza until it's delivered.)

One more innovation: if you are not at your home or office, no problem. The company has now created over 200,000 Hotspots, outdoor locations where you can have your pizza delivered instead.[5]

How is this pizza/IT business doing? From when Doyle took over as CEO in March 2010 to April 2018, the Domino's market cap exploded, increasing from $816 million to nearly $10.5 billion. This made it one of the top performers of the last decade.[6] If Domino's were in the S&P 500, it would be number three in terms of performance, trailing only Netflix (+3,095%) and United Rentals (+1,814%). When Doyle took over, Domino's stock was trading at $8.76.[7] As of this writing, the stock is now trading at $401.55 per share.[8]

To successfully call your shot requires strategic clarity,

high levels of focus, a measure of grit, and a massive dose of leadership.

EXPAND OWNERSHIP

Intentionally increase participation and engagement through the creation of actual or psychological ownership.

In 1983, Springfield Remanufacturing Company (SRC) was on the ropes. The stock price was at ten cents per share. The company was not going to survive. Enter Jack Stack and a group of fellow employees with no experience running a business, who bought the company.[9]

Stack was convinced there was a future for the company. He decided to expand the ownership and responsibility for turning around the organization. His strategy was to create a "business of business people." To do this, the culture had to change, and the employees would be the ones to change it.

How did the team approach this daunting challenge? Its playbook contained three big ideas:

- Know and teach the rules (of business).
- Follow the action and keep score.
- Provide a stake in the outcome.

Stack and his team began an aggressive business literacy program. They expected every employee to understand and impact the company's financial statements. One tactic they employed was reimagining the role of the accounting team. Jack commissioned the team to move from being historians to becoming teachers. He said, "Don't tell us what happened; teach us how to make things happen." Corporate financials were distributed on a regular basis to help all employees follow the action. And the company created its Employee Stock Ownership Plan to create a stake in the outcome.

Years ago, I had the opportunity to visit Springfield and learn from Stack and his team. I have never encountered a greater sense of ownership from frontline employees. Engagement and business literacy were evident at all levels of Stack's organization.

I recall a conversation with a longtime frontline worker whose job was to carefully extract and clean a very small part buried deep inside the engines the company was charged to rebuild. The employee beamed with pride as he told me each part he could successfully salvage would save the company twenty-five cents.

I wonder how many employees in the world are excited to save their companies twenty-five cents. The cumulative effect of this level of engagement and ownership has created a remarkable culture. In turn, the culture has enabled spectacular performance. This is what High Performance Cultures do!

Even though SRC's core business of rebuilding engines hasn't changed, it has expanded its holdings to include logistics, distribution, and warehousing. Over the last thirty years, SRC's performance has been astonishing. Its culture change and the resulting performance improvements have created tremendous value. SRC's stock price increased 348,000 percent over thirty years. Here's how that math works: $1,000 invested in Berkshire Hathaway in 1983 would have been worth $113,000 in 2013; the same amount invested in SRC would have been worth $3.4 million. I guess it is true, a "business of business people" will outperform a business of employees.[10]

How much ownership do your employees feel? What would happen if they had a high degree of ownership? The potential gains for most organizations are staggering. Improvements include retention, engagement, innovation, customer satisfaction, profitability, and more. This is one move I think every organization should consider regardless of stock price. I do not know of a better way to run an organization. Real or psychological ownership will enhance the culture and performance of your organization.

CHANGE THE GAME

Fundamentally challenge and alter an industry's norms by reimagining long-held assumptions and practices.

Mayo Clinic was founded in 1864 by William Worrall Mayo. For decades, the hospital has been rated as one of the top medical facilities in the world, often occupying the top spot in rankings. It has built a reputation for world-class care and a willingness to tackle the most challenging cases. However, as most would agree, the healthcare industry is in need of transformation. The confluence of rising costs and growing inequities around the world regarding access to quality healthcare, complexity, specialization, silos, advances in technology, and more must be addressed.

Dr. Gianrico Farrugia is the president and CEO of Mayo Clinic. He wants his hospital to change the game in healthcare. In a 2020 interview, he said, "Leaders cannot just respond to what's happening. They have to anticipate where things are, where things are going, and then they have to chart a course for their organization to get them there."[11]

His strategy is built on three imperatives: cure, connect, and transform. I'll let the doctor explain for himself.

Cure is all about our traditional core of Mayo Clinic, the mission of providing team-based medical expertise for patients with complex or serious conditions, provided to people who are either local or are willing to travel to come for their cures. I very much believe that with the right structure, with the right people, with the right space, with the right technology, we truly can get to new or better cures. But in order to cure, we also need to connect, and we need to transform.

That second word, *connect*, is about dealing with health care's complexity, its fragmentation, its inaccessibility. This is the time. We have the right digital technology to innovate, to simplify health care for patients. This is where we will develop those physical and virtual tools so we can connect with patients when and wherever they need it and in ways that they're so accustomed to in other spheres of their life but not in health care.

The last one is *transform*, and that's about building Mayo Clinic as a platform, moving all of Mayo's data onto a platform so we can extract new knowledge from it. That will mean that we now can deliver digital knowledge and insights globally. We can provide world-class health care globally while at the same time informing our own practice. We're moving forward in three main areas: home hospital, clinical data analytics, and advanced digital diagnostics. The platform will help us connect with patients more effectively, deliver care when our patients need it, and do it in a way that still provides that unparalleled experience with the highest quality and always with that human touch that health care so much continues to need.[12]

When doing what you have done in the past is not the way forward, you need to chart a new course. If true transformation is your aim, you may even need to change the game. If you are successful, you might just change your world.

CONNECT THE DOTS
Link two or more strategic objectives and increase the odds of accomplishing both.

The war was raging. Men were dying by the tens of thousands. President Abraham Lincoln was in battle physically, emotionally, and literally with the challenge of maintaining the Union. Many would question his motives—was this really a war over slavery? According to Lincoln, no ... at least not in the beginning.

Horace Greeley was a reformer, abolitionist, and editor of an influential newspaper, the *New-York Tribune*. He wrote an editorial critical of the president and his war policies. A few days later, on August 22, 1862, the President wrote the following in his response to Greeley.

> As to the policy I "seem to be pursuing" as you say, I have not meant to leave any one in doubt ...
>
> My paramount object in this struggle is to save the Union, and is not either to save or to destroy slavery. If I could save the Union without freeing any slave I would do it, and if I could save it by freeing *all* the slaves I would do it; and if I could save it by freeing some and leaving others alone I would also do that ...
>
> I have here stated my purpose according to my view of *official* duty; and I intend no modification of

my oft-expressed *personal* wish that all men everywhere could be free.

Yours,

A. Lincoln.[13]

As the war progressed, the president found a way to legitimately and constitutionally link his "personal wish" with his "official duty" to preserve the Union: the Emancipation Proclamation.

Lincoln determined that emancipating slaves in rebellious states was "warranted by the Constitution" as "a fit and necessary war measure for suppressing said rebellion." He reasoned that slave labor was used to support the Confederate army and therefore gave the Confederacy a distinct advantage. Lincoln believed freeing these slaves would weaken the Confederate army, justifying the Emancipation Proclamation as an act of "military necessity" valid under the Constitution.

On September 22, 1862, Lincoln released the preliminary Emancipation Proclamation, which warned the states in rebellion that if they did not rejoin the Union by January 1, 1863, their slaves would be freed.

As the war continued into the new year, the Emancipation Proclamation took effect in the ten rebellious states: Alabama, Arkansas, Florida, Georgia, Louisiana, Mississippi, North Carolina, South Carolina, Texas, and Virginia. "All persons held as slaves within said designated States, and parts of States, are, and henceforward shall be free," declared Lincoln in the Proclamation.[14] From this point forward, the war was about preserving the Union *and* freeing the slaves.

We call Lincoln's strategy "Connect the Dots." When you link two or more items together, one may be considered the primary objective and the other(s) secondary. Regardless, by linking them, you may increase the odds of success for your secondary initiative if the primary one is more compelling or achievable. Lincoln was able to connect freeing enslaved people to his primary objective of preserving the Union. How could you use this approach to connect two or more cultural change initiatives in your organization?

THINK SMALL
Identify a seemingly narrow, and often simple, behavior that will create a positive ripple effect in the culture.

In October 1987, investors and stock analysts were ready to meet Alcoa's new CEO, Paul O'Neill. Many were not sure what to expect from this former Washington insider who began his career working for the US Department of Veterans Affairs as a computer systems analyst in 1961. His career trajectory had later taken him to the US Office of Management and Budget in 1967. Some in the room were probably wondering if he would be the right leader for Alcoa, a company steeped in history and bureaucracy. Founded in 1888 and one of the world's largest producers of aluminum, the company was well entrenched and slow to change. Could a man coming out of the largest bureaucracy in the world break the one he would inherit at Alcoa? All of this uncertainty intensified as O'Neill began his remarks: "I want to talk to you today about worker safety." Firsthand accounts of the moment indicate the audience was confused; this was not the way these meetings typically began.

O'Neill continued, "Every year, numerous Alcoa workers are injured so badly they miss a day of work. Our safety record is better than the general American workforce, especially considering that our employees work with metals that are 1,500 degrees and machines that can rip a man's arm off. But it's not good enough. I intend to make Alcoa the safest company in America. I intend to go for zero injuries."[15]

When someone raised a question about inventory in their aerospace division, he responded, "I'm not certain you heard me. If you want to understand how Alcoa is doing, you need to look at our workplace safety figures."

You may look at this as an obscure way to change a culture, and maybe so. But in the case of Alcoa, this approach worked. Over O'Neill's tenure, Alcoa dropped from 1.86 annual injury-caused lost work days per hundred workers to 0.2. By 2012, the rate had fallen to 0.125.[16]

What impact did improved safety have on the culture and performance? The company's market value increased from $3 billion in 1986 to $27.53 billion in 2000, while net income increased from $200 million to $1.484 billion.[17]

To "think small" should not be assumed to generate small outcomes. The trick is to find the right behavior or activity to focus on. For our organization, two simple words, "My pleasure," have had a similar impact as safety did at Alcoa. These two words, spoken countless times every day by hundreds of thousands of team members around the country, have elevated our service, enhanced our performance, and changed our culture.

TAKE IT OFF BROADWAY
Deliberately use small, often out-of-sight experiments to test and learn during a change effort.

Culture change is often thought of as introducing big, bold, game-changing ideas that immediately have a transformative effect on an organization. Although this is theoretically possible, culture change is most often the result of many, much smaller interventions. Many times, these adjustments do not even begin under the bright lights for all to see. Sometimes they begin as an experiment far from the big stages on Broadway.

Laszlo Bock was the senior vice president of People Operations at Google. He and his team were huge fans of experiments—interventions they could plan, execute, and evaluate against control groups and repeat if necessary. Many of these experiments were conducted under Google's Optimize Your Life program. The program's stated goal was to help employees be healthy, wealthy, and wise.[18] Let's take a quick look at a few examples of the team's work.

Healthy. Google wants to create a culture that contributes to the life expectancy of its employees. The company wants to say with full integrity, "Work at Google, and you will live longer!" A big focus has been on diet and nutrition. With almost 70 percent of Americans being obese or overweight, Google sees this as an area of opportunity.

One series of Laszlo's experiments focused on reducing caloric intake from Google's cafés and micro-kitchens. First, Laszlo and his team tried sharing caloric and other health-related information on posters and signage. There was no change in behavior. Next, they attempted to limit food options; that didn't go over well, either. Then they repositioned the healthy options in clear packaging and put the candy in labeled opaque containers. In *one* office, over seven weeks, the employees consumed 3.1 million fewer calories. This is something Google has now replicated in other offices.

Wealthy. Google realized many of its employees were not

participating in its 401(k) retirement program—the company matches 50 percent of employees' contributions, up to the maximum allowed by the IRS. And, as Google knew from research, the number-one variable (outside of total lifetime income) impacting accumulated savings at retirement is how early someone begins saving. So Laszlo and his team decided to do an experiment.

They crafted and sent four different emails to those not participating in the program and monitored the results. What they learned was all the emails helped increase participation and saving rates; however, some messages were more effective than others. This form of "A/B testing" allowed them to continue to refine the message to maximize enrollment.

The increased contributions from their test cases alone, assuming an 8 percent return, will result in an additional $260,000 per employee at retirement. Google now sends these messages out annually and continues to experiment with new language. Googlers are saving more and more every year.

Wise. Google really wants employees to be more productive and to stay with Google longer. These objectives have led to many experiments with new hires (called Nooglers). Here's just one example:

The Sunday night before a new employee started work, their supervisor would receive an email with a five-point checklist.

1. Have a role-and-responsibilities conversation.
2. Connect your Noogler with a peer buddy.
3. Help your Noogler build their social network.
4. Set up onboarding check-in meetings once a month for six months.
5. Encourage open dialogue.

This experiment resulted in Nooglers getting up to speed 25 percent faster than those whose managers did not receive the nudge.[19]

At any given time, you will find Google experimenting with numerous ideas to enhance its culture. You can do the same. You don't have to start big, and you probably shouldn't for some of your ideas. Take it off Broadway, test it, measure the results, and test it again if needed. Once you have something that works, you can share the practice across your entire organization.

When do you take a project off Broadway? This approach to improvement is one you'll use when there isn't a high degree of urgency. Here are a few questions to help you apply this approach.

What are the culture-enhancing projects you could begin to experiment with off Broadway? How could you build a low-cost, low-resolution prototype? Who are the emerging leaders who would benefit from the opportunity to lead a project like this? How can you free up some time and resources to support these future-oriented culture enhancements?

PLAYER OR PRETENDER?

In this last section, we reviewed seven strategies you can use to enhance your culture or course-correct. Of course, you can create your own list of interventions as well. Regardless of how many strategies you formulate, they will all have at least one thing in common: the difference maker in all of them will be the leader. As we have tried to establish throughout this book, *leaders animate culture.* Therefore, you have to decide if you are ready to step up and take your turn. Are you a player or a pretender?

The answer to this lies squarely in your willingness to address toxins and the maladies they birth. Granted, to Adapt is only one of the three rules of the game, but it is the rule that determines the longevity and vitality of your culture. Your response also determines to a large extent how long you, as the leader, will be allowed to continue to play the game. Be a player!

YOUR MOVE...

What facet of your culture represents your greatest challenge or opportunity? Which of the previous countermeasures do you think would offer your greatest chance of success?

GAME ON!

ENDURANCE

If you're a leader, a fellow that other fellows
look to, you've got to keep going.
—**Ernest Shackleton**

The year was 1909, and Ernest Shackleton's second expedition to Antarctica was over. He and three companions had set their sights on reaching the South Pole, but a mere ninety-seven miles from their prize, the men were forced to turn back for lack of rations. Their retreat was a race against death itself.

Disappointed but not defeated, Shackleton returned to England as a hero. He was knighted by the King, wrote a book, and began traveling the world, sharing the story of his adventures. Biographer Alfred Lansing described Shackleton this way:

In ordinary situations, Shackleton's tremendous capacity for boldness and daring found almost nothing worthy of its pulling power; he was a Percheron draft horse harnessed to a child's wagon cart. But in the Antarctic— here was a burden which challenged every atom of his strength.[1]

This "capacity for boldness" almost guaranteed Shackleton would once again go south. The only questions remaining: When would he go, and what would be his aim?

In 1912, Roald Amundsen from Norway would do what Shackleton could not—he became the first man to reach the South Pole. With this opportunity gone, Shackleton turned his ambition to the only feat left: to cross Antarctica by land.

AN AUDACIOUS GOAL

Even as Shackleton learned of Amundsen's success, his mind had long before turned to a new possibility. In March 1911, a full year before Amundsen's accomplishment, he wrote to his wife, "I feel that another expedition unless it crosses the continent is not much."[2]

This single sentence became the essence of Shackleton's next adventure. Joined by his crew of twenty-seven men (plus one stowaway, who became the ship's steward), sixty-nine dogs, and a tomcat named Mrs. Chippy, he boarded the *Endurance* and departed on the Imperial Trans-Antarctic Expedition on August 1, 1914.

The trip across the Atlantic took two months. This was the first significant amount of time at sea for the *Endurance*, and for some of the crew, this would be their first expedition. The ship was reportedly the strongest ship of its day, with its wooden walls several feet thick at places to withstand the ice it would soon encounter.

The plan was for Shackleton and his crew to approach the Weddell Sea, traveling west, while another ship approached from the east. The *Endurance* landing party, led by Shackleton, would then begin to traverse the continent, while the other ship would send its land party toward the South Pole, leaving provisions along the way. In theory, when Shackleton's team moved to and past the Pole, they would find the supplies left by their companions and meet them on the other side of the continent on the Ross Sea, south of New Zealand.[3]

The plan was audacious—it was Shackleton.

TRAPPED

Unfortunately, the world will never know if the plan would have worked. On December 5, the *Endurance* left South Georgia Island; this would be the last time the crew would set foot on dry ground for 497 days.

Just two days later, the ship encountered the barrier of ice that surrounded the continent. The crew demonstrated great skill in navigating the floes, large sheets of floating ice sometimes hundreds of feet thick. The *Endurance* continued to move southward as the way forward became increasingly perilous. Then, on January 18, gale-force winds pressed the giant pieces of ice against each other and the ship. The convergence of millions of tons of ice created colossal pressure. The crew was helpless. In the blink of an eye, the ship was taken captive by the frozen sea.

When describing the moment of incapacitation, Thomas Orde-Lees, a member of the crew, said the *Endurance* was "frozen like an almond in the middle of a chocolate bar."[4] In that moment, Shackleton's goal changed from traversing the continent to survival.

Shackleton was a leader willing to confront reality. He confided in Frank Worsley, the ship's captain, "The ship can't live in this, Skipper . . . It may be a few months, and it may be only a question of weeks, or even days . . . but what the ice gets, the ice keeps."[5]

CULTURE BUILT ON PURPOSE

Shackleton was keenly aware of the culture he wanted to create on the *Endurance* long before the crew ever set sail. Let's start with his Aspiration. From an operational perspective, his expedition was about crossing the continent of Antarctica on foot—but crossing was the *goal*, not his *purpose*.

There has been much written about Shackleton's confidence and his ego. Many have wondered if he could have attempted what he did without them. However, I don't believe the voyage of the *Endurance* was about Shackleton's self-aggrandizement. As I read about the preparation for this trip, I believe the expedition was the perfect confluence of Shackleton's personal giftedness, passion, and love of his country and adventure. As is often the case, your cultural Aspiration may be an amalgamation of your personal talents, gifts, passions, and dreams.

These elements combined to create the higher sense of purpose Shackleton needed to build his crew and his culture. Not only was Shackleton's Aspiration grounded in purpose, but he also knew the importance of selection in creating the culture he wanted. Others have said he could pick a rose from a thousand thorns, including the ability to recruit loyal, dependable men from the rougher side of life. His skills were certainly tested, as he had over five thousand applicants for the fifty available positions.[6]

Here is journalist Michael Smith's assessment of some of Shackleton's key recruits.

His crew would be anchored by stalwarts like Frank Wild, Tom Crean, and Ernest Joyce. For the most part, these men and others like them were rootless, living out of a kitbag or drifters looking for a role in life. But they proved to be invaluable members of the team, particularly in the most challenging circumstances when lives were at risk. Wild and Crean, for example, served on a total of eight Antarctic expeditions between them. Wild, who went on five expeditions, accompanied Shackleton on his "furthest south" in 1909. Irish-born Crean was among the last to see Captain Scott alive a few miles from the South Pole in 1912, [and] saved the life of Lt. Evans on the epic return march.[7]

Not only did Shackleton pick experienced men, but he also selected some future explorers with no experience at all. Regardless of their experience, he knew the values all the men would need to embrace for his organization to be successful. Their ultimate survival and success rested on optimism, patience, imagination, and courage. He felt if he could find men who already possessed these attributes, they could be explorers.

CULTURE SHINES IN CRISIS

Once trapped in the ice, Shackleton knew he would have to work to maintain the culture and the morale of his men. Uncertain regarding when or if the ship would be released from the ice, he continued to assign responsibilities to the crew for maintaining the ship. Sailors swabbed decks, scientists collected specimens from the ice, and others hunted for seals and penguins when fresh meat, a protection against scurvy, ran low.[8] The crew lived aboard the ice-bound ship for about eight months until she could withstand the pressure no more.

On October 27 at 5 PM, Shackleton gave the order to abandon ship, but according to all accounts, this was not a surprise to the men. They could see what the ice was doing to the vessel, and despite their best efforts, they could not stop the relentless onslaught of millions of pounds of ice.

On November 1, 1915, the ship was crushed, and the men were stranded. In the process of moving to the ice, Shackleton and the men had to determine which items to salvage. Frank Hurley, the ship's photographer, made the painful decision to leave behind four hundred of his negatives, keeping only 120. Leonard Hussey was about to leave his banjo behind, but Shackleton ordered him to keep it. He knew the men would need the music to lift their spirits.

The problems with their temporary home were many, not the least of which, they were 1,200 miles from any form of civilization. Their first attempt to make their way to safety was to walk toward land, but this plan was abandoned after the men managed just seven and a half miles in seven days.

"There was no alternative but to camp once more on the floe and to possess our souls with what patience we could till conditions should appear more favorable for a renewal of the attempt to escape," wrote Shackleton.[9]

In the midst of it all, Shackleton kept his cool. He knew the men were watching his every move—not just what he said, but how he said it. He would continue to be their rock and their undisputed leader.

As author and historian Nancy Koehn observes, "He knew

that each day, his presence had huge impact on the men's mindsets. He managed his own emotional intelligence—to use a modern term—to keep his own courage and confidence high; when these flagged, he never let his men know."[10]

The ice slowly drifted farther north, and on April 7, 1916, the peaks of Clarence and Elephant Islands came into view, giving Shackleton's men hope. Shackleton wrote in his diary: "The floe has been a good friend to us, but it is reaching the end of its journey and is liable at any time now to break up."[11]

CHEAT DEATH ... AGAIN

In April 1916, understanding fully the cost of inaction—having experienced the floe literally breaking apart underneath them— the crew boarded the three lifeboats that had been taken off the *Endurance*. The men left the floating ice and started an arduous voyage to uninhabited Elephant Island. Seven long days later, they arrived. Miraculously, everyone survived this phase of the journey.

Understanding their new location on the island was an improvement but still untenable, Shackleton, Worsley, and four others set out in one of the lifeboats, the *James Caird*, to seek help from a whaling station on South Georgia more than eight hundred miles away. For sixteen days, they fought the sea and raging winds until they finally landed on the island. Unfortunately, the stormy weather had pushed the boat off course, and now they were on the opposite side of the island from the whaling station.[12]

They knew their battered boat was no longer seaworthy and could not make the journey around the island, so their only remaining option to reach the station was to cross the island on foot. Two of the men were too sick to cross the island and one was needed to care for them, so, only Shackleton, Worsley, and Crean would make the attempt.

The route from the shore to the station was across virtually impassable terrain, and the island had never been crossed before. This next phase of the journey would require another herculean demonstration of strength, stamina, and sheer willpower.

The men had no map and few supplies. They carried only enough rations for three days, an extra pair of socks, forty-eight matches, one lamp, and a small cooker. They used screws from the *Caird* to fashion spikes on the bottom of their boots to minimize slipping on the snow and ice. They took no tents or sleeping bags because they would not sleep—they would march.

At one point in the darkness, the terrain became so steep, they decided to slide into the abyss—with full knowledge this might be the last decision they'd ever make. They could not see where they were going; all they knew was they were out of options. The three literally slid down the mountain on seats fashioned of rope. They descended three thousand feet in about three minutes, and again they survived!

Thirty-six hours after they began their trek, the three men arrived at the whaling station in Stromness, South Georgia.

SHACKLETON TO THE RESCUE

The final leg of this epic adventure was to rescue the entire crew still marooned on Elephant Island. While the men waited, fear and anxiety grew as winter approached. Yet every day, in the face of a potentially devastating future, Frank Wild, the man

Shackleton had left in charge, issued the call for everyone to "lash up and stow" their belongings. "The Boss may come today!"[13]

Shackleton made two failed attempts to reach his men. Both times, he was rebuffed by the same pack ice that had taken the *Endurance*. But on August 30, 1916, on his third attempt, he finally broke through, and 128 days after Shackleton had departed from the island on the *James Caird*, the crew of the *Endurance* was rescued.

Every member survived.

WHY SHACKLETON?

As I thought about how to close this book, I knew many leaders would benefit from seeing another leader in action. I needed to find someone who did the things I've advocated throughout this book in challenging circumstances and yet prevailed. And someone whose success could be directly linked to the culture they had built. Shackleton came immediately to mind.

Shackleton was intensely focused on culture, and his organization reflected his Aspiration perfectly. He wanted a culture that embodied the values of optimism, patience, imagination, and courage, and that is exactly what he built. Every culture bears the fingerprints of its leader.

Based on all accounts, Shackleton was also a great leader. Someone people wanted to follow. I think we all need people we can look up to—we all need heroes. Perhaps Shackleton can become one of yours.

Finally, I wanted to end with the story of Shackleton's epic journey because of his family motto: *Fortitudine vincimus.* By endurance we conquer.

High Performance Cultures are not built overnight—they require a never-ending pursuit. As far as I know, the journey is never easy, but when the days are long and the wins are elusive, I hope you will dig down deep and find the endurance you need to do something great. The world needs your leadership.

READY PLAYER ONE

It's not about winning; it's about playing.
—Parzival

W ade Watson is focused. His pulse quickens with anticipation. He is preparing to enter the OASIS, the virtual
world he visits often. Once inside, he becomes Parzival, a cool kid with a cool car and growing confidence. Out-
fitted with his full-body interactive gaming suit and headset, he
resembles a futuristic take on his avatar's namesake, the medie-
val knight in full armor known for his search for the Holy Grail.

It's the year 2045, and Wade is an orphaned teen living with
his aunt in an impoverished situation within a dystopian world.
As the unlikely hero of a plot that unfolds in two worlds—the
real world and a virtual one—his survival in both realities is
based on how well he plays a game James Halliday, the creator of
the OASIS, has left behind. In the OASIS, Wade has access to
unimaginable possibilities beyond his everyday reach. The only
problem: none of it is real. That is, *almost* none of it.

This is *Ready Player One*, the film adaptation of Ernest

Cline's best-selling science fiction novel of the same name, directed by Steven Spielberg.

Why the title *Ready Player One*? In the early days of video arcades, the last words a player would read before a game began were "Ready, player one." Cline loved the phrase. To him, it was a clear signal: "All right, now you're entering another world."[1]

As Cline's story begins, Wade is playing his own game—for himself and by himself. But as his journey progresses, the limits of this "go it alone" mentality are slowly revealed as he encounters extreme hardship and personal loss. Through his pain, he ultimately discovers the power of community and an ever-expanding sense that he has more control over his world than he wants to believe. These lessons, combined with Wade's personal integrity, forge a powerful force for good.

To exercise his newfound agency, Parzival and his friends in the OASIS search for the three keys that will give them ultimate control of their virtual world. With the keys, they envision unlocking a better future—both online and off. Of course, there is opposition at every turn.

Like Parzival, most leaders in our world today are also trying to create a better world (aka culture). I put you squarely in this camp—or you wouldn't have read this book. Every page you've read has been intended to give you the rules and moves you will need to succeed as you build your own magic circle.

I have intentionally not made the clues as cryptic as those Wade and his friends encounter on their journey. You don't even need to *search* for any mythical keys. The leaders we have featured in this book have given you the only three rules you'll need and a head start on the moves to build or transform your culture.

HIGH PERFORMANCE CULTURE

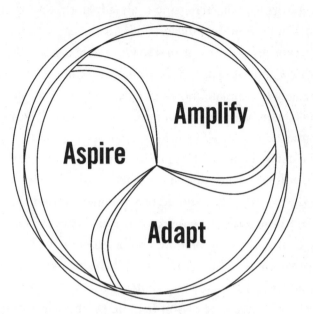

Aspire: *Share your hopes and dreams for the culture.*
Amplify: *Ensure the cultural Aspiration is reinforced continuously.*
Adapt: *Always work to enhance the culture.*

However, having the rules handed to you is not enough. Just like in the OASIS, leaders in our reality face stiff opposition as they attempt to create a better world. Today, the culprit is complex and often nuanced. Facets of the resistance can come disguised as growth, complexity, busyness, distractions, fear, fatigue, aimlessness, and many other forms. However, the greatest obstacle to creating a High Performance Culture is a lack of focused leadership attention.

Parzival's ultimate success and the better world he is able to create is predicated on a single moment: he chooses to lead. Most likely, you already have a seat at the table. If you are part of an existing organization, the game is already underway. Only you can determine your next move.

This entire book was created to illuminate one big idea: *leaders animate culture.* Culture is your work, your responsibility, and your opportunity. Just like Wade, you may see yourself as an unlikely hero. Don't sell yourself short. You were born to play this game!

The consequences of not playing are clear. Left unattended, culture will not evolve to a better place—cultures without leadership devolve, dissolve, and destroy themselves from the inside. They succumb to one or more of the maladies we discussed. However, disease, deterioration, and death are not your destiny. If you play by the rules, you can build your own unique and sustainable High Performance Culture.

At this point, some of you may be troubled by a lingering question: Can I really create a magic circle to enable our people and our organization reach our full potential?

I believe you can. Countless other leaders have done this important work before you. Success leaves clues, and we have captured and distilled many of those into the pages you've just read. Be thoughtful and intentional. While the rules are few, the moves are infinite. Make the moves your own. Dedicate yourself to the task at hand, and do not give up.

Let's close with a return to the youthful wisdom of Parzival. I think there is a hidden gem in his observation about the OASIS—something that might even enhance your own Aspiration: "People come to the OASIS for all the things they can do, but they stay for all the things they can be."[2]

Imagine what might happen if people said this about your

culture. If people came to your organization because of what they could do and then stayed because of who they could become, I think you would be well on your way to creating your own High Performance Culture—a place known for its unity; life-giving, soul-enriching work; and elite levels of performance.

Ready, Player One!

Acknowledgments

A project of this scope and magnitude requires years of work by a large team. During our journey together, I have thanked them privately on numerous occasions, but here is my opportunity to thank them publicly.

Core Team. Erin Myers, Michael Barry, Amanda Bhalla, Mike Johnson, Michelle Jia, Yuri Zaitsev, Ellie Thornton, Danny Chapman, Erin Weissert, Gia Schutzer, Mike Fleming, Jessica Everett, and Hannah Weisman—thank you!

These were the primary players, thinkers, and creators behind this work. Together, we slogged through a tremendous amount of information in search of something that would serve leaders around the world. Every push, pull, and challenge made this work better. The insights you have just read can be attributed to the collective tenacity and spirit of this team. As we often said in our discussions, all we're trying to do is help you change your world. I am confident this talented group of people has provided you with the opportunity to do just that.

Reviewers and editors. Mike Johnson, Katie Dickman, Lydia Choi, Janice Rutledge, Leah Baxter, Randy Gravitt, Brittany Miller, Donna Miller, Justin Miller, Emi Gragnani, Darya Fields, and Charmaine Bather made this book possible. Without their guidance and tough love along the way, we would have nothing worth publishing. Thank you!

MJ, your patience, coaching, and attention to detail were greatly appreciated! You are a better storyteller than I am, and the folks who read this book should thank *you* for your tireless efforts to make this book an accurate and compelling reflection of the leaders and companies we studied.

Interviewees. For confidentiality reasons, we cannot list all the leaders we interviewed by name. In an attempt to acknowledge them, we have listed the companies they represent.

Accenture

Alexion Pharma, Inc.

Amazon

An Design (Kyoto, Japan)

Charles Schwab

Chemours Brazil (Brazil)

Chick-fil-A

Clemson University

Coca-Cola

Delta

Denise Lee Yohn, Inc.

Disney

Dunnhumby

FedEx

Field Museum

Google

Hilton

Joyful Planet

Kautex Textron (Germany)

Lee Company

Marriott

May & Baker (Nigeria)

MetLife (Japan)

Microsoft

Morning Brew

Netflix

NewSpring Church

Nike

North Illinois Food Bank

NYC Department of Education

Oracle

Play

Porsche

Professional Children's School (NYC)
Qualtrics
RaceTrac
Ross School of Business
Royal DSM
Salesforce
Southwest Airlines
Stanford University
Starbucks
Steelcase
Student Maid
The Edge Group
Tiger Brands (South Africa)
Tuhu (China)
UiPath (India)
United Airlines
University of Michigan, Stephen M. Ross School of Business
Untold (Kenya)
Vontier
Wellstar Health System

Additional research participants. More than six thousand people from ten countries took time to complete a survey or participate in a focus group. Your insights were instrumental in this work. Thank you!

Designers. Brigid Pearson, Lindsay Miller, and Jordan Koluch. I love great design! It is a treat to work with people who can make words on a page look spectacular. Thank you!

Publishing team. Matt Holt, Alex Field, Mallory Hyde, and team, thanks for believing together we can change the world!

Additional Resources

I trust you found value in what you've just read. Some of you have discovered your next steps to begin realizing the untapped potential in your organization. Congratulations! For others, you may need additional information or assistance.

One of the resources our team created to help you activate the ideas you just read about is the *Culture Rules* Field Guide. If you would like a **FREE** digital copy, use the QR code below. This 100+ page guide contains scores of tactics, additional case studies, helpful questions, and more.

CULTURE RULES FIELD GUIDE

Regardless of what's next for you, my team and I have created many other resources to help you on your journey. We have additional books, field guides, assessments, videos, and more to help you build your own High Performance Culture and High Performance Organization.

Please let me know how I can serve you or your team in the future. Visit my website, LeadEveryDay.com, for rich content, free resources, links to my social channels, and more. You can also call or text me at 678-612-8441. I'm here to cheer you on!

Notes

INTRODUCTION

1. Johan Huizinga, *Homo Ludens: A Study of the Play-Element in Culture* (Brooklyn: Angelico Press, 2016).

2. "*This Is Water* by David Foster Wallace (Full Transcript and Audio)," Farnam Street, accessed July 26, 2022, https://fs.blog/david-foster-wallace-this-is-water/.

BEFORE YOU PLAY

1. "The Flywheel Effect," Jim Collins website, accessed July 26, 2022, https://www.jimcollins.com/concepts/the-flywheel.html.

2. Brent Gleeson, "9 Navy SEAL Sayings That Will Improve Your Organization's Ability to Lead Change," *Forbes*, July 23, 2018, https://www.forbes.com/sites/brentgleeson/2018/07/23/9-navy-seal-sayings-that-will-improve-your-organizations-ability-to-lead-change/?sh=1b0a410864d4.

WHY PLAY THE GAME?

1. John Kotter, "Does Corporate Culture Drive Financial Performance?," *Forbes*, February 10, 2011, https://www.forbes.com/sites/johnkotter/2011/02/10/does-corporate-culture-drive-financial-performance/?sh=24dbce147e9e.

2. Chris Gagnon, Elizabeth John, and Rob Theunissen, "Organizational Health: A Fast Track to Performance Improvement," *McKinsey Quarterly*, September 7, 2017, https://www.mckinsey.com/business-functions/people-and-organizational-performance/our-insights/organizational-health-a-fast-track-to-performance-improvement.

3. "Aligned Companies Significantly Outperform Their Peers," LSA 3x Organizational Alignment Research, LSA Global, accessed July 26, 2022, https://lsaglobal.com/insights/proprietary-methodology/lsa-3x-organizational-alignment-model/.

4. State of the American Workplace Report, Gallup, 2015–16.

5. Naina Dhingra, Andrew Samo, Bill Schaninger, and Matt Schrimper, "Help Your Employees Find Purpose—or Watch Them Leave," McKinsey & Company, April 5, 2021, https://www.mckinsey.com/business-functions/people-and-organizational-performance/our-insights/help-your-employees-find-purpose-or-watch-them-leave.

6. Ibid.

7. "Culture Over Cash? Glassdoor Multi-Country Survey Finds More Than Half of

Employees Prioritize Workplace Culture Over Salary," Glassdoor, July 10, 2019, https://about-content.glassdoor.com/en-us/workplace-culture-over-salary/.

A NEW GAME

1. Matt Anderson, "Ford's Five-Dollar Day," The Henry Ford, January 3, 2014, https://www.thehenryford.org/explore/blog/fords-five-dollar-day/.

2. David J. Trowbridge, "Prosperity and Its Limits," *United States History*, Volume 2, accessed August 15, 2022, https://2012books.lardbucket.org/books/united-states-history-volume-2/s09-01-prosperity-and-its-limits.html.

3. Rosabeth Moss Kanter, *Rosabeth Moss Kanter on the Frontiers of Management* (Boston: Harvard Business School Press, 1997).

4. "A History of Honoring," Proud to Honor, Ford website, accessed July 26, 2022, https://www.ford.com/proud-to-honor/history.

5. Mike Arnholt and Tim Keenan, "Foreign Invasion: Imports, Transplants Change Auto Industry Forever," WardsAuto Industry News, May 1, 1996, https://www.wardsauto.com/news-analysis/foreign-invasion-imports-transplants-change-auto-industry-forever.

6. "Alan Mullaly," International Air & Space Hall of Fame, San Diego Air & Space Museum, accessed July 26, 2022, https://sandiegoairandspace.org/hall-of-fame/honoree/alan-mulally.

7. "Epiphany in Dearborn," *Economist*, December 9, 2010, https://www.economist.com/briefing/2010/12/09/epiphany-in-dearborn.

8. Marshall Goldsmith, "I Know Less Than You Do—and It's Okay!," LinkedIn, January 2, 2018, https://www.linkedin.com/pulse/i-know-less-than-you-do-its-okay-dr-marshall-goldsmith.

9. Sarah Miller Caldicott, "Why Ford's Alan Mulally Is an Innovation CEO for the Record Books," *Forbes*, June 25, 2014, https://www.forbes.com/sites/sarahcaldicott/2014/06/25/why-fords-alan-mulally-is-an-innovation-ceo-for-the-record-books/?sh=176a4d637c04.

10. Carmine Gallo, "Alan Mulally, Optimism, and the Power of Vision," *Forbes*, April 25, 2012, https://www.forbes.com/sites/carminegallo/2012/04/25/alan-mulully-optimism-and-the-power-of-vision/?sh=618d93537abb.

11. Marli Guzzetta, "The 4 Keys to One of the Biggest Turnarounds in Business History," *Inc.*, October 12, 2017, https://www.inc.com/marli-guzzetta/how-alan-mulally-turned-ford-around-inc5000.html.

12. NYSE, *Ford Motor Company*, retrieved August 11, 2022, https://finance.yahoo.com/quote/F/history/.

13. Tushar Vakil, "Organization Culture Change Example—Alan Mulally Ford Turnaround Story," New Age Leadership, accessed July 26, 2022, https://newageleadership.com/organizational-culture-change/.

14. Lewis Carroll, *Alice's Adventures in Wonderland* (New York: Macmillan, 1865).

USE THE FORCE

1. Dictionary.com, "ethos (n.)," accessed August 24, 2022, https://www.dictionary.com/browse/ethos.

2. Andrea Huspeni, "6 Things You Need to Know About How Netflix Built Its Powerful Culture," *Entrepreneur*, June 29, 2017, https://www.entrepreneur.com/article/296209.

3. *Knowledge at Wharton* staff and Patty McCord, "Learning from Netflix: How to Build a Culture of Freedom and Responsibility," *Knowledge at Wharton*, May 29, 2018, https://knowledge.wharton.upenn.edu/article/how-netflix-built-its-company-culture/.

4. Reed Hastings, "Culture," SlideShare, August 1, 2009, https://www.slideshare.net/reed2001/culture-1798664.

LEAVE NO DOUBT

1. Matthew Johnston, "5 Companies Owned by Pepsi," Investopedia, March 14, 2021, https://www.investopedia.com/articles/markets/122215/top-5-companies-owned-pepsi-pep.asp.

2. Mary Jane Credeur, "Pepsi Passes Coke in Market Value," *Seattle Times*, December 13, 2005, https://www.seattletimes.com/business/pepsi-passes-coke-in-market-value/.

3. "Indra Nooyi—Biography & Career Accomplishments," ThomasNet, accessed July 26, 2022, https://www.thomasnet.com/articles/other/indra-nooyi-biography-career/.

4. Indra K. Nooyi and Vijay Govindarajan, "Becoming a Better Corporate Citizen," *Harvard Business Review* (March–April 2020), https://hbr.org/2020/03/becoming-a-better-corporate-citizen.

5. Ibid.

6. Ibid.

7. Briana Boyington, Emma Kerr, and Sarah Wood, "20 Years of Tuition Growth at National Universities," *US News & World Report*, September 17, 2021, https://www.usnews.com/education/best-colleges/paying-for-college/articles/2017-09-20/see-20-years-of-tuition-growth-at-national-universities.

8. Higher Ed Dive Team, "A look at trends in college consolidation since 2016," Higher Ed Dive (website), August, 12, 2022, https://www.highereddive.com/news/how-many-colleges-and-universities-have-closed-since-2016/539379/.

9. Michael M. Crow and William B. Dabars, *Designing the New American University* (Baltimore: Johns Hopkins University Press, 2015).

10. "ASU Charter, Mission and Goals," About page, Arizona State University, accessed July 26, 2022, https://newamericanuniversity.asu.edu/about/asu-charter-mission-and-goals.

11. Michelle Goldberg, "This Is What Happens When You Slash Funding for Public Universities," *The Nation*, May 19, 2015, https://www.thenation.com/article/archive/gentrification-higher-ed/; "Facts and Figures," Arizona State University website, accessed August 18, 2022, https:// www.asu.edu/about/facts-and-figures.

12. Emma Greguska, "ASU Ranked No. 1 in Innovation for 6th Year by *US News and World Report*," Arizona State University News, September 13, 2020, https://news.asu.edu/20200913-asu-news-us-news-world-report-no-1-innovation-sixth-year.

13. Ibid.

14. "Purpose and Vision," Coca-Cola Company website, accessed July 26, 2022, https://www.coca-colacompany.com/company/purpose-and-vision.

15. "Our Credo," Johnson & Johnson website, accessed July 26, 2022, https://www.jnj.com/credo/.

16. About Netflix home page, accessed July 26, 2022, https://about.netflix.com/en.

17. "Ferrari," HEC Business Game website, accessed July 26, 2022, https://www.hecbusinessgame.com/ferrari.

DREAM BIG DREAMS

1. "Address at the Sorbonne in Paris, France: 'Citizenship in a Republic,'" Theodore Roosevelt, The American Presidency Project, accessed July 26, 2022, https://www.presidency .ucsb.edu/documents/address-the-sorbonne-paris-france-citizenship-republic.

2. "The IKEA vision and values," IKEA About Us page, accessed August 19, 2022, https:// www.ikea.com/us/en/this-is-ikea/about-us/the-ikea-vision-and-values-pub9aa779d0.

3. "Declaration of Interdependence," Whole Foods Market Mission and Values Page, accessed July 26, 2022, https://www.wholefoodsmarket.com/mission-values/declaration-interdependence.

4. "Who We Are," Amazon About Us page, accessed July 26, 2022, https://www.aboutamazon .com/about-us.

5. "Mission and Vision," Habitat for Humanity website, accessed August 19, 2022, https:// www.habitat.org/about/mission-and-vision.

6. "About Feeding America," Feeding America About Us page, accessed July 26, 2022, https://www.feedingamerica.org/about-us.

7. "Read Martin Luther King Jr.'s 'I have a Dream' Speech in Its Entirety," NPR, last modified January 14, 2022, https://www.npr.org/2010/01/18/122701268/i-have-a-dream -speech-in-its-entirety.

8. "Address at Rice University on the Nation's Space Effort, September 12, 1962," John F. Kennedy: Speeches, John F. Kennedy Presidential Library and Museum, accessed July 26, 2022, https://www.jfklibrary.org/archives/other-resources/john-f-kennedy-speeches /rice-university-19620912.

LEAD WITH VALUES

1. Nate Dvorak and Bailey Nelson, "Few Employees Believe in Their Company's Values," Gallup, September 13, 2016, https://news.gallup.com/businessjournal/195491/few -employees-believe-company-values.aspx

2. Ibid.

3. "Culture and Values," Starbucks Careers page, accessed July 26, 2022, https://www .starbucks.com/careers/working-at-starbucks/culture-and-values/.

4. "Developing a New Expression of Our Company Culture," DSM Integrated Annual Report 2020, accessed July 26, 2022, https://annualreport.dsm.com/ar2020/report-by -the-managing-board/people/focusing-on-our-people-through-the-pandemic/developing -a-new-expression-of-our-company-culture.html.

5. Dharmesh Shah, "The HubSpot Culture Code: Creating a Company We Love," HubSpot Blogs, accessed July 26, 2022, https://blog.hubspot.com/blog/tabid/6307/bid/34234/the -hubspot-culture-code-creating-a-company-we-love.aspx.

6. "Join Us," Headspace website, accessed August 22, 2022, https://www.headspace.com /join-us.

HIT REFRESH

1. "Microsoft founded," This Day in History April 04, History.com, last modified April 1, 2020, https://www.history.com/this-day-in-history/microsoft-founded.

2. "History of Microsoft," Los Angeles Times Archives, April 4, 2000, https://www.latimes .com/archives/la-xpm-2000-apr-04-fi-15769-story.html.

3. Tim Worstall, "Microsoft's Market Share Drops from 97% to 20% in Just Over a Decade," *Forbes*, December 13, 2012, https://www.forbes.com/sites/timworstall/2012/12/13/microsofts-market-share-drops-from-97-to-20-in-just-over-a-decade/?sh=ba3b3b751cf7.

4. Tristan Louis, "The Ballmer Era Ends. What to Make of It?," *Forbes*, September 28, 2013, https://www.forbes.com/sites/tristanlouis/2013/09/28/ballmer-era-ends/?utm_source=followingdaily&utm_medium=email&utm_campaign=20130929&sh=1df335ff23a1.

5. Sydney Finkelstein, "The Worst CEOs of 2013," *BBC Worklife*, December 12, 2013, https://www.bbc.com/worklife/article/20131212-the-worst-ceos-of-2013.

6. Jonathan Rettinger, "Microsoft's 4 Biggest Problems," *HuffPost*, August 1, 2014, https://www.huffpost.com/entry/microsofts-four-biggest-problems_b_5641212.

7. Kelly Clay, "Steve Ballmer Steps Down from Microsoft Board," *Forbes*, August 19, 2014, https://www.forbes.com/sites/kellyclay/2014/08/19/steve-ballmer-steps-down-from-microsoft-board/?sh=2c387c521c90.

8. "'Hit Refresh' by Satya Nadella," Microsoft News page, accessed July 26, 2022, https://news.microsoft.com/hitrefresh/.

9. Satya Nadella, Greg Shaw, and Jill Tracie Nichols, *Hit Refresh: The Quest to Rediscover Microsoft's Soul and Imagine a Better Future for Everyone* (New York: HarperCollins, 2017).

10. Anna Johnston, "Microsoft: Instilling a Growth Mindset," *London Business School Review*, no. 3 (2018), https://herminiaibarra.com/wp-content/uploads/2019/07/IBARRA_et_al-2018-London_Business_School_Review.pdf.

11. Kathleen Hogan, "Screen In to Diversity Your Workforce," LinkedIn, September 7, 2016, https://www.linkedin.com/pulse/screen-diversify-your-workforce-kathleen-hogan.

12. Ibid.

13. Chantrelle Nielsen and Natalie McCullough, "How People Analytics Can Help You Change Process, Culture, and Strategy," *Harvard Business Review*, May 17, 2018, https://hbr.org/2018/05/how-people-analytics-can-help-you-change-process-culture-and-strategy.

14. Jason Aten, "Microsoft Just Dethroned Apple as the World's Most Valuable Company with a Brilliant Strategy: Be Boring," *Inc.*, October 31, 2021, https://www.inc.com/jason-aten/microsoft-just-dethroned-apple-as-worlds-most-valuable-company-with-a-brilliant-strategy-be-boring.html.

15. NasdaqGS, Microsoft Corporation stock quote, retrieved August 11, 2022, https://finance.yahoo.com/quote/MSFT/history/.

16. "Amplify," Merriam-Webster, accessed July 26, 2022, https://www.merriam-webster.com/dictionary/amplify.

FOLLOW THE LEADER

1. Nate Barksdale, "8 Surprising Facts About Alexander the Great," History, last modified August 29, 2018, https://www.history.com/news/eight-surprising-facts-about-alexander-the-great.

2. Flavius Arranius, *The Anabasis of Alexander; or the History of the Wars and Conquests of Alexander the Great*, translated by E. J. Chinnock (London: Hodder and Stoughton, 1883).

3. Ibid.

4. Ibid.

5. "Marc Benioff," Salesforce Leadership page, accessed July 26, 2022, https://www.salesforce.com/company/leadership/bios/bio-benioff/.

6. Dan Pontefract, "Salesforce CEO Marc Benioff Says the Business of Business Is Improving the State of the World," *Forbes*, January 7, 2017, https://www.forbes.com/sites/danpontefract/2017/01/07/salesforce-ceo-marc-benioff-says-the-business-of-business-is-improving-the-state-of-the-world/?sh=5b4a6a847eb0.

7. Kate Vidinsky, "Marc Benioff Announces $100 Million Gift to Build New Children's Hospital at Mission Bay," University of California San Francisco News & Media page, June 23, 2010, https://www.ucsf.edu/news/2010/06/100979/marc-benioff-announces-100-million-gift-build-new-childrens-hospital-mission.

8. "Pledge 1%," Salesforce, accessed July 26, 2022, https://www.salesforce.org/about/pledge/.

TELL ME A STORY

1. "The Chauvet Cave Paintings," Bradshaw Foundation Rock Art Archives, accessed July 26, 2022, https://www.bradshawfoundation.com/chauvet/chauvet_cave_paintings.php.

2. Brian Dean, "Social Network Usage & Growth Statistics: How Many People Use Social Media in 2022?," BackLinko, October 10, 2021, https://backlinko.com/social-media-users.

3. Vanessa Boris, "What Makes Storytelling So Effective for Learning?," Harvard Business Publishing Corporate Learning Blog, December 20, 2017, https://www.harvardbusiness.org/what-makes-storytelling-so-effective-for-learning/.

4. Paul J. Zak, "Why Your Brain Loves Good Storytelling," *Harvard Business Review*, October 28, 2014, https://hbr.org/2014/10/why-your-brain-loves-good-storytelling.

5. Maria Popova, "The Storytelling Animal: The Science of How We Came to Live and Breathe Stories," *The Marginalian* (blog), May 3, 2012, https://www.themarginalian.org/2012/05/03/the-storytelling-animal-jonathan-gottschall/.

6. "Marshall Ganz | Public Narrative," YouTube video, 16:14, posted by "California Teachers Association," November 2, 2015, https://www.youtube.com/watch?v=g7CW_10C7lQ.

7. "Therapeutic Reminiscing and Storytelling: Helping Your Loved One with Alzheimer's to Reconnect with the World," North Woods Village website, June 6, 2017, https://www.northwoodsmemorycare.com/therapeutic-storytelling-helping-alzheimers-reconnect/.

8. Carmine Gallo, "Steve Jobs: The World's Greatest Business Storyteller," *Forbes*, October 8, 2015, https://www.forbes.com/sites/carminegallo/2015/10/08/steve-jobs-the-worlds-greatest-business-storyteller/?sh=3e6ebe3413f0.

9. Ibid.

10. https://www.victorialabalme.com/

CREATE TOMORROW TODAY

1. Jeff James, "Optional or Operational? The Case for Great Training," LinkedIn, February 28, 2018, https://www.linkedin.com/pulse/optional-operational-case-great-training-jeff-james.

2. David Novak, "Recognizing Employees Is the Simplest Way to Improve Morale," *Harvard Business Review*, May 9, 2016, https://hbr.org/2016/05/recognizing-employees-is-the-simplest-way-to-improve-morale.

3. Ibid.

4. Valarie Daunt and Vicky Menzies, "Recognition Programmes," Deloitte website, accessed August 18, 2022, https://www2.deloitte.com/ie/en/pages/deloitte-private/articles/recognition-programmes.html.

5. Justin Rapp, "5 Things You Need to Know About the Blue Legacy Name Tag," Disney Parks Blog, March 7, 2022, https://disneyparks.disney.go.com/blog/2022/03/5-things-you-need-to-know-about-the-blue-legacy-name-tag/.

6. "Tradition," Merriam-Webster, accessed July 26, 2022, https://www.merriam-webster.com/dictionary/tradition.

7. Jeff Benedict, "Clemson Football: Homefield Advantage Is Still Real in 2020," Rubbing the Rock, FanSided Network, September 18, 2020, https://rubbingtherock.com/2020/09/18/clemson-football-homefield-advantage/.

8. Mark Schlabach, "Gift from Death Valley Became 'Death Valley' Tradition," ESPN, September 14, 2007, https://www.espn.com/college-football/columns/story?columnist=schlabach_mark&id=3017840.

9. Jack Welch, *Jack: Straight from the Gut* (New York: Warner Books, 2001).

WIN WITH PEOPLE

1. "Decades Before Moneyball, the Dallas Cowboys Used Advanced Stats to Win Super Bowls," *FiveThirtyEight* Sports, December 17, 2014, https://fivethirtyeight.com/features/cowboys-and-indian-fivethirtyeight-films-signals/.

2. Phil Savage and Ray Glier, *4th and Goal Every Day: Alabama's Relentless Pursuit of Perfection* (New York: St. Martin's Press, 2017).

3. Sydney Hunte, "Nick Saban Reveals What He Tells Recruits Looking to Commit to Alabama," Saturday Down South, accessed July 26, 2022, https://www.saturdaydownsouth.com/alabama-football/nick-saban-reveals-what-he-tells-recruits-looking-to-commit-to-alabama/.

4. Dan Schawbel, "Hire for Attitude," *Forbes*, January 23, 2012, https://www.forbes.com/sites/danschawbel/2012/01/23/89-of-new-hires-fail-because-of-their-attitude/?sh=5dce530c137a.

5. Ibid.

6. Shane McFeely and Ben Wigert, "This Fixable Problem Costs US Businesses $1 Trillion," Gallup, March 13, 2019, https://www.gallup.com/workplace/247391/fixable-problem-costs-businesses-trillion.aspx.

7. Sundiatu Dixon-Fyle, Kevin Dolan, Vivian Hunt, and Sara Prince, "Diversity Wins: How Inclusion Matters," McKinsey & Company, May 19, 2020, https://www.mckinsey.com/featured-insights/diversity-and-inclusion/diversity-wins-how-inclusion-matters.

8. Derek Anderson, "The Story Behind Qualtrics, the Next Great Enterprise Company," TechCrunch, March 2, 2013, https://techcrunch.com/2013/03/02/the-story-behind-qualtrics-the-next-great-enterprise-company/; NasdaqGS, Qualtrics International Inc. stock quote, retrieved August 18, 2022, https://finance.yahoo.com/quote/xm/.

9. "Organizational Core Values: Definition, Benefits, and Examples," Qualtrics Resources page, accessed July 26, 2022, https://www.qualtrics.com/experience-management/employee/organizational-core-values/.

ALIGN BY DESIGN

1. "More Than Half of Employees Globally Would Quit Their Jobs If Not Provided Post-Pandemic Flexibility, EY Survey Finds," EY press release, May 12, 2021, https://www.ey

.com/en_us/news/2021/05/more-than-half-of-employees-globally-would-quit-their-jobs
-if-not-provided-post-pandemic-flexibility-ey-survey-finds.

2. Ashley Abramson, "Burnout and Stress Are Everywhere," *Monitor on Psychology* 53, no. 1
(2022), https://www.apa.org/monitor/2022/01/special-burnout-stress.

3. John Kounios and Mark Beeman, "How Incentives Hinder Innovation," *Behavioral Scientist*, September 3, 2015, https://behavioralscientist.org/how-incentives-hinder-innovation
-creativity/.

4. Dan Ariely, "What's the Value of a Big Bonus?," *New York Times*, November 19, 2008,
https://www.nytimes.com/2008/11/20/opinion/20ariely.html.

5. Nic Paton, "Performance-Related Pay Doesn't Encourage Performance," *Management-Issues*,
June 25, 2009, https://www.management-issues.com/news/5640/performance-related
-pay-doesnt-encourage-performance/.

CHAMPIONS CHANGE, TOO

1. Frank Keating, "How the Original All Blacks Went Down in the Annals of History,"
Guardian, November 2, 2010, https://www.theguardian.com/sport/blog/2010/nov/03/all
-blacks-new-zealand-1905.

2. James Kerr, *Legacy* (London: Constable & Robinson, 2013).

3. Ibid.

4. Andy Bull, "The Making of an All Black: How New Zealand Sustains Its Rugby Dynasty,"
Guardian, September 11, 2015, https://www.theguardian.com/sport/blog/2015/sep/11
/all-blacks-how-new-zealand-sustains-its-rugby-dynasty.

5. Kerr, *Legacy*.

6. Kerr, *Legacy*.

7. Kerr, *Legacy*.

8. "The Haka," All Blacks home page, accessed July 26, 2022, https://www.allblacks.com
/the-haka/.

9. "Teams," All Blacks home page, accessed July 26, 2022, https://www.allblacks.com
/teams/all-blacks/.

10. Hitesh Bhasin, "Nike Advertising: Techniques Used by Nike in Advertising," Marketing91,
August 29, 2020, https://www.marketing91.com/nike-advertising/.

SCALE YOUR LISTENING

1. "How Many Emails Are Sent Every Day? Top Email Statistics for Businesses," Templafy
Blog, August 9, 2020, https://www.templafy.com/blog/how-many-emails-are-sent-every
-day-top-email-statistics-your-business-needs-to-know/.

2. Peter Cheney, "The Rise of Japan: How the Car Industry Was Won," *Globe and Mail*,
November 5, 2015, https://www.theglobeandmail.com/globe-drive/adventure/red-line
/the-rise-of-japan-how-the-car-industry-was-won/article27100187/.

3. "Who Created Kaizen?," Creative Safety Supply, accessed July 26, 2022, https://www
.creativesafetysupply.com/qa/kaizen/who-created-kaizen.

4. Yuzo Yasuda, *40 Years, 20 Million Ideas: The Toyota Suggestion System* (Cambridge, MA:
Rudra Press, 1990).

5. "Leading Car Companies in 2020 and 2021, Based on Worldwide Light Vehicle

Sales," Statista, accessed July 26, 2022, https://www.statista.com/statistics/268977/global-leading-car-companies-based-on-worldwide-vehicle/.

6. "A True Toy Story: LEGO's Incredible Turnaround Tale," The CFO Centre Blog, October 6, 2017, https://www.cfocentre.com/us/true-toy-story-legos-incredible-turnaround-tale-2/.

7. Jena McGregor, "Brick by Brick: The Man Who Rebuilt the House of Lego Shares His Leadership Secrets," *Washington Post*, December 8, 2016, https://www.washingtonpost.com/news/on-leadership/wp/2016/12/08/brick-by-brick-the-man-who-rebuilt-the-house-of-lego-shares-his-leadership-secrets/.

8. "Leadership Secrets from Lego," Business Management Daily, June 1, 2017, https://www.businessmanagementdaily.com/48879/leadership-secrets-from-lego/.

9. McGregor, "Brick by Brick."

10. "RaceTrac Petroleum," *Forbes*, last modified November 23, 2021, https://www.forbes.com/companies/racetrac-petroleum/?sh=56e8e7505340.

11. Peter F. Drucker, "The Effective Decision," *Harvard Business Review* (January 1967), https://hbr.org/1967/01/the-effective-decision.

MEASURE WHAT MATTERS

1. "BCBS Health Index," Blue Cross Blue Shield website, accessed July 26, 2022, https://www.bcbs.com/the-health-of-america/health-index.

2. Personal interview with the author, May 6, 2021.

DON'T BREATHE

1. E. A. Wrigley, "Energy and the English Industrial Revolution," *Philosophical Transactions of the Royal Society* 371, no. 1986 (March 13, 2013), doi:10.1098/rsta.2011.0568.

2. Christal Pollock, "The Canary in the Coal Mine," *Journal of Avian Medicine and Surgery* 30, no. 4 (December 2016): 386–91, doi:10.1647/1082-6742-30.4.386.

3. Ibid.

4. Kat Eschner, "The Story of the Real Canary in the Coal Mine," *Smithsonian*, December 30, 2016, https://www.smithsonianmag.com/smart-news/story-real-canary-coal-mine-180961570/.

5. "WHO Releases New International Classification of Diseases (ICD 11)," World Health Organization news release, June 18, 2018, https://www.who.int/news/item/18-06-2018-who-releases-new-international-classification-of-diseases-(icd-11).

6. "ADP Research Institute Sets International Benchmark for Employee Engagement with Its 19-Country Global Study of Engagement," ADP Newsroom, June 14, 2019, https://mediacenter.adp.com/2019-06-14-ADP-Research-Institute-Sets-International-Benchmark-for-Employee-Engagement-with-its-19-Country-Global-Study-of-Engagement.

7. Mike Isaac, "Uber Fires 20 Amid Investigation into Workplace Culture," *New York Times*, June 6, 2017, https://www.nytimes.com/2017/06/06/technology/uber-fired.html.

8. Nick Lioudis, "The Collapse of Lehman Brothers: A Case Study," Investopedia, last modified January 30, 2021, https://www.investopedia.com/articles/economics/09/lehman-brothers-collapse.asp.

9. John Dobson, "Enron: The Collapse of Corporate Culture," in *Enron and World Finance: A Case Study in Ethics*, eds. Paul H. Dembinski, Carole Lager,

Andrew Cornford, and Jean-Michel Bonvin (New York: Macmillan, 2006), 193–205, doi:10.1057/9780230518865_12.

10. Troy Segal, "Enron Scandal: The Fall of a Wall Street Darling," Investopedia, last modified November 26, 2021, https://www.investopedia.com/updates/enron-scandal -summary/.

11. Peter Drucker, "The Rise of the Knowledge Society," *Wilson Quarterly* 17, no. 2 (1993), https://go.gale.com/ps/i.do?p=AONE&u=googlescholar&id=GALE|A13905270&v=2.1 &it=r&sid=googleScholar&asid=c29b7aed.

12. Avery Hartmans, Sarah Jackson, and Áine Cain, "The Rise and Fall of Elizabeth Holmes, the Former Theranos CEO Found Guilty of Wire Fraud and Conspiracy, Whose Sentencing Has Now Been Delayed," *Business Insider*, July 13, 2022, https://www.businessinsider.com /theranos-founder-ceo-elizabeth-holmes-life-story-bio-2018-4.

13. Ibid.

MASTER CLASS

1. "Explosion of the Space Shuttle *Challenger*: Address to the Nation, January 28, 1968, by President Ronald W. Reagan," NASA History Office, accessed July 26, 2022, https:// history.nasa.gov/reagan12886.html.

2. Francisco Polidoro Jr., "Why Organizations Forget What They Learn from Failures," *Harvard Business Review*, February 29, 2016, https://hbr.org/2016/02/why-organizations-forget -what-they-learn-from-failures.

3. Bill Taylor, "How Domino's Pizza Reinvented Itself," *Harvard Business Review*, November 28, 2016, https://hbr.org/2016/11/how-dominos-pizza-reinvented-itself.

4. Ibid.

5. "What Are Domino's Hotspots?," Domino's About Pizza page, accessed July 26, 2022, https://www.dominos.com/en/about-pizza/delivery-hotspots/.

6. Lisa Fu, "Domino's CEO Rides Off into the Sunset After Leading One of the Greatest Turn Arounds of All Time (DPZ)," Yahoo! Finance, April 27, 2018, https://finance.yahoo .com/news/domino-apos-ceo-rides-off-185500944.html.

7. Taylor, "How Domino's Pizza Reinvented Itself."

8. MarketWatch Domino's Pizza Inc. Overview, accessed July 26, 2022, https://www.market watch.com/investing/stock/dpz.

9. "Our Culture of Employee Ownership," SRC of Lexington, Inc., accessed July 26, 2022, https://srclexington.com/about/our-culture/.

10. Bo Burlingham and Jack Stack, *The Great Game of Business, Expanded and Updated: The Only Sensible Way to Run a Company* (New York: Crown Business, 2013).

11. Gianrico Farrugia and Thomas H. Lee, "Cure, Connect, Transform: Three Mayo Clinic Strategy Components for Servant Leaders," *NEJM Catalyst Innovations in Care Delivery*, July 9, 2020, https://catalyst.nejm.org/doi/full/10.1056/CAT.20.0416.

12. Ibid.

13. "Letter to Horace Greeley," Speeches and Writings, Abraham Lincoln Online, accessed July 26, 2022, https://www.abrahamlincolnonline.org/lincoln/speeches/greeley.htm.

14. "Transcript of the Proclamation," National Archives Online Exhibits: The Emancipation

Proclamation, accessed July 26, 2022, https://www.archives.gov/exhibits/featured
-documents/emancipation-proclamation/transcript.html.

15. Rodd Wagner, "Have We Learned the Alcoa 'Keystone Habit' Lesson?," *Forbes*, January 22, 2019, https://www.forbes.com/sites/roddwagner/2019/01/22/have-we-learned-the-alcoa
-keystone-habit-lesson/?sh=6b6e7be758ba.

16. Drake Baer, "How Changing One Habit Helped Quintuple Alcoa's Income," *Business Insider*, April 9, 2014, https://www.businessinsider.com/how-changing-one-habit
-quintupled-alcoas-income-2014-4.

17. Charles Duhigg, *The Power of Habit: Why We Do What We Do in Life and Business* (New York: Random House, 2012).

18. Laszlo Bock, *Work Rules! Insights from Inside Google That Will Transform How You Live and Lead* (New York: Hachette, 2015).

19. Ibid.

ENDURANCE

1. Alfred Lansing, *Endurance: Shackleton's Incredible Voyage* (New York: Basic Books, 2014).

2. Ibid.

3. "History of *Endurance*," Endurance22 History page, accessed July 26, 2022, https://endurance22.org/history-of-endurance.

4. Kieran Mulvaney, "The Stunning Survival Story of Ernest Shackleton and His *Endurance* Crew," History.com Stories page, March 9, 2022, https://www.history.com/news/shackleton
-endurance-survival.

5. "Excerpt from *The Endurance*," Penguin Random House Canada, accessed July 26, 2022, https://www.penguinrandomhouse.ca/books/1850/the-endurance-by-caroline-alexander
/9780375404030/excerpt.

6. Michael Smith, "How Shackleton Recruited His Men," Shackleton.com Blog, January 4, 2020, https://shackleton.com/blogs/articles/shackleton-recruitment.

7. Ibid.

8. Nancy F. Koehn, "Leadership Lessons from the Shackleton Expedition," *New York Times*, December 24, 2011, https://www.nytimes.com/2011/12/25/business/leadership-lessons
-from-the-shackleton-expedition.html.

9. Mulvaney, "The Stunning Survival Story."

10. Koehn, "Leadership Lessons."

11. Mulvaney, "The Stunning Survival Story."

12. Ibid.

13. Ibid.

READY PLAYER ONE

1. Mansoor Mithaiwala, "Why Is the Movie Called *Ready Player One* Anyway?," Screen Rant (website), July 24, 2018, https://screenrant.com/ready-player-one-title-name-explained
-book-movie/.

2. *Ready Player One*, directed by Steven Spielberg (2018; Warner Bros. Pictures), movie.

Index

About the Author

Mark Miller is a business leader, best-selling author, and communicator.

Mark started his Chick-fil-A career working as an hourly team member in 1977. In 1978, he joined the corporate staff working in the warehouse and mail room. Since then, he has provided leadership for corporate communications, field operations, quality and customer satisfaction, training and development, leadership development, and more. During his tenure with Chick-fil-A, the company has grown from seventy-five restaurants to almost three thousand locations, with annual sales approaching $20 billion.

He began writing over twenty years ago when he teamed up with Ken Blanchard, coauthor of *The One Minute Manager,* to write *The Secret: What Great Leaders Know and Do.* The book you now hold in your hands is Mark's eleventh. With over one million books in print in more than twenty-five languages, Mark's global impact continues to grow.

In addition to his writing, Mark enjoys encouraging and equipping leaders. Over the years, he's traveled to dozens of countries teaching for numerous international organizations.

Mark is also an avid photographer who loves shooting in some of the most remote places on the planet. Past adventures have taken him to the jungles of Rwanda in search of silverback gorillas, across the Drake Passage to Antarctica, and to several high-altitude destinations, including Mount Kilimanjaro and Everest Base Camp.

Married to Donna, his high school sweetheart, for over forty years, they have two sons, Justin and David; a daughter-in-law, Lindsay; and three amazing grandchildren, Addie, Logan, and Finn.